ENDORSEMENTS

———

Make no mistake: The lines are drawn, and the battle is at hand. This time, it is a fight for the very fabric of America. There has never been a more critical moment for our country. We are poised on the brink of utter greatness, with a rabid left that wants to tear it all down.

Carl Higbie is a true American patriot on and off the battlefield, who fought for this country before and will inspire you to fight for the best country in the history of the world, under the best president in the history of America. The time is now! Carl's fight for America is bolder than ever in *Crisis of Culture* - a no-holds-barred gut punch to the regressive left's war on America, our childrens' futures, and our President.

DR. GINA LOUDON, CONSERVATIVE
COMMENTATOR & AUTHOR

———

What I love about Carl beyond his loyalty and warrior spirit is if he gets knocked down, he gets back up. We all trip and fall in life but his perseverance is second to none.

Carl is a great American who should inspire many.

ROBERT O'NEILL, U.S. NAVY SEAL & AUTHOR

———

Carl is a friend of mine and I love his unique perspective on what is happening in our culture right now. He volunteered to serve this country and protect our freedoms, so he knows firsthand how to bridge what we're seeing in America today with what he saw on the battlefield while bringing common sense solutions. This is the book I think every American should read!

WAYNE DUPREE, NEWSMAX'S TOP
50 INFLUENTIAL BLACK REPUBLICANS

———

CRISIS OF CULTURE

THE POLITICAL BATTLEFIELD OF THE NEW CIVIL WAR

CARL HIGBIE

TACT16AL

Crisis of Culture: The Political Battlefield of the New Civil War

First Edition

Published by Tactical 16, LLC
Colorado Springs, CO

ISBN: 978-1-943226-30-6 (ebook)
ISBN: 978-1-943226-31-3 (paperback)
ISBN: 978-1-943226-32-0 (hardback)

Printed in the United States of America

FOREWORD

I've been in politics for more than fifty years. I've worked in various capacities from the top staff level of the White House to political roles within the Nixon, Reagan and Bush administrations. I was privileged to serve as Chief White House Advisor and Campaign Manager for President Ronald Reagan's successful 1984 re-election campaign against Walter Mondale when he won forty-nine out of fifty states. I also served as the Co-Chairman of the National Republican Congressional Campaign Committee and served as the Chief Political Advisor to the House Republican leadership. I have had leadership roles in eight other presidential campaigns and had oversight for hundreds of other campaigns at the state and local levels.

I have had the unique privilege to serve as the chief political advisor for leaders at both ends of Pennsylvania Avenue.

It's fair to say, I've been around the block. I've seen my fair share of infighting and dirty tricks. Politics is not a game for the faint of heart. With that said, I have not seen an environment like this in my entire career. Bomb threats, street violence, destruction of campaign headquarters and a total hostility in the political environment by the left and liberal media who are on a crusade to destroy anyone who supports President Trump or is associated with the Trump administration. In many cases the efforts are to personally destroy individuals beyond the bounds of what we have observed in the past. The bitterness, polarization and anger are dangerous to our extraordinary democracy.

I first met Carl in 2015 at Fox News as we both campaigned in support of President Trump. Before the election, we worked together at the Great America PAC where I had the opportunity to get to know him well, both professionally and personally. Much like our president, I have been impressed with Carl's passion, conviction and commitment. Having served with distinction as a Navy SEAL, he is a proven man of courage and not one to run away from an argument or conflict. He will fight, no matter the personal consequence, for the issues he believes in and leave nothing behind on the battlefield. His ability to get punched and punch back is one of the key things that will save our country. I can unequivocally say the narrative the media has promulgated about him is false. The fact that the left and mainstream media actively seek to personally destroy honorable men and women for the crime of simply holding a different opinion is something that all rational people must oppose.

In Carl's book he outlines many of the issues we face as a nation today and provides emotion-free assessment and suggestions for how we can move forward. You can agree with all, some or none of what he has to say, but I encourage everyone to read it and to learn from his story. As a society, it is essential we all maintain perspective and take the personal enmity out of our national discussion.

Ed Rollins

TACTICAL 16

One of the fundamental principles I live by is to pay it forward. One hundred percent of the proceeds of this book go back to the publisher, Tactical 16, which specializes in working with veterans, first responders and their friends and families to publish their writing as a means to tell their story and for self-therapy.

I have gotten to know the Tactical 16 president and founder, Erik Shaw, during this process. Mr. Shaw, a US Army combat veteran who started the company in 2012, discovered the therapeutic value of writing while crafting his memoir, *Brave Rifles*. Erik Shaw wanted to share his discovery with others who suffered from post-traumatic stress and to provide honest and fair services to authors who have amazing stories but didn't have a chance in hell of ever getting a book deal.

Tactical 16 understands the therapeutic value that writing provides. They work with their authors throughout the entire process, including after their books are printed, to help them succeed. Understanding the ins and outs of getting a book published can be difficult. Tactical16 is committed to helping their authors achieve their goals through a cost-effective and supportive approach. The mission of

Tactical 16 is to preserve and share their authors' victories, tragedies, triumphs and entertaining stories.

The victor always writes the history, but oftentimes that history is written by someone that neither served nor lived during the conflict. I chose Tactical 16 because they are on a mission to write the history of America's conflicts by those who experienced it—all of it, the messy and chaotic, the mind blowing and the tragic, the stories of good people in dangerous situations and the wrong people that made conditions perilous, as well as the politics and policies that impacted organizations at a fundamental level for better or worse. Tactical 16 presents these stories through the eyes of civilian first responders and the men and women of the armed forces affected by the nation's longest war.

Aside from helping to preserve history and assisting those with PTS during the writing process, Tactical 16 has published books in children's, business, leadership and fiction genres. They continue to look for those unique stories that are uncommonly told by civilians, veterans and first responders young and old.

The name Tactical 16 has two parts. Tactical refers to the armed forces, police, fire and rescue communities. The "16" is the number of acres destroyed on September 11, 2001, at Ground Zero.

My hope is that the proceeds of this book will help men and woman who put foot to ass for this country when she called. I encourage other members of my community to tell their story.

INTRODUCTION

Have you ever said something that you wish you could take back? I have, and if you pay any attention to CNN you'll know why. We all experience things in our lives that both solidify and change who we are. The turmoil around my resignation from a high-level presidential appointment I experienced in early 2018 was no different: it reinforced my conservative views but also led me to try to understand some of the opposing views we have in society today.

We are in a civil war that is not fought with guns but through the media and by those who will stop at nothing to take down President Trump. This time it is a fight between political ideology rather than a single issue such as slavery. And just like the Civil War under President Lincoln, this war is only being fought by very loud and relatively small "armies" on either side, while most Americans are stuck in the middle just tiring to survive. But as the proverbial bullets fly past us and the "causalities"—me, David Sorenson, Anthony Scaramucci, Michael Flynn, Sebastian Gorka, Ximena Barreto, Rosanne Barr and many more—add up (at least on the conservative side), we need to take a step back. As the left has moved toward totalitarianism and socialism, the two sides have gotten so far apart that the success of this nation is not sustainable at this tempo. You will see in this book that I try not to use Republican or Democrat but rather liberal or conservative to define groups because that touches the person rather than a political party.

When I left the military, I will admit I was extremely firm, even angry in my views and not interested in compromise; I was just interested in winning the argument at any cost. Certain views on homosexuality were burned into me by the sexual abuse I endured as a child and reinforced in an environment where that was not accepted during the vast majority of my service. In military training, in order to help us cope with the intense combat we would see as Navy SEALs, we were psychologically conditioned to identify those we were fighting as less than human to facilitate our effectiveness as machines. This was over simplified to a hatred of Islam, and it even made me move away from my own religion of Christianity as a side effect.

Entitlement programs were not liked in the military either. In many cases, people on federal assistance make more than our junior soldiers who put their lives on the line and that didn't sit well in the military community.

Fast forward to present: I have made a significant effort to walk a mile in other people's shoes that I didn't previously understand—or even cared to. This has changed some of my views and solidified others. I am still a staunch conservative and Trump supporter, but I have gained the wisdom to be able to disagree with someone and still respect him or her. Some people will disagree with the opinions in this book, but before you offer a challenge, ask yourself if you have walked a mile in the other person's shoes? Because I likely have prior to putting it on paper. I will not compromise on something that is a fact because by nature it is not a changeable position. I will, however, lay out my solutions to address issues that are not so black and white. This book is my attempt to pass that on to the country I love more than most will ever know.

―――――

Now on my third book, I don't feel the need to re-write my biography. I have always been a results-oriented person—achievement is paramount. As my friend Dan and I always say, "Bourbon, cigars, results." This type of thinking has been what propels me to succeed. Where others struggle and fail, I find strength to persevere. This attitude allowed me to stand out as a wrestler, Navy SEAL, business owner, author, Congressional candidate, media pundit and a presidential appointee, all before I was 35 years old, but not without struggles and failures along the way, and I learned from each one.

I will address many difficult issues in this book, even ones I still struggle with personally. This is not done out of hate; it is out of love for America and my desire to fix the problems I see. To do so, I am perfectly willing to offend people, even those who are my strong base of support, because I am less concerned with who is offended and more concerned about who is affected. I am tired of society ignoring facts because they hurt someone's feelings. It is time we address the elephant(s) in the room and how we got to this divided state that was on clear display with the Kavanaugh hearings.

I have always loathed talkers, people who believe action constitutes achievement, which is largely why I despise our current government's system as I do. And I'm not alone on either side of the aisle. I have equally little patience for entitlement, which most of my generation is guilty of. Too many people think that they are entitled to equal status—regardless of their own merits—simply because someone else has achieved something desirable.

Humility is the most important trait one can have; if you enter any situation confidently, yet humble, there is nothing you cannot achieve. Do every job, no matter how insignificant, to the best of your ability. As a state champion wrestler in high school, I learned these lessons the hard way; the moment you slack off or get cocky, you make mistakes. Never underestimate your opponent; I have done this before and lost. In my television career, too, I have gone into debates unprepared and maybe a little bit too confident; getting smacked down on national TV can be a bit humbling. But I have learned valuable lessons through these instances and this is why I encourage people to strive out of their comfort zones because a failure can be the greatest lesson one can learn, and it is under that premise that I wrote this book.

WALK A MILE IN MY SHOES: THE CAMPAIGN

I have been politically active since the release of my first book in 2012 while still on active duty; I was a lightning rod after criticizing President Obama for governing failures. But the announcement of Donald Trump's presidential run was about to launch me into the center of the most controversial political race and time ever. Having been a veteran of the national cable news networks as a frequent commentator for three years, I had a good base knowledge of the way media worked and how to make it work in your favor; but that knowledge did not prepare me for what I was about to experience over the next eighteen months.

At the time I had never met Mr. Trump, but when he came down the escalator to launch his campaign I knew he was going to win. I had previously stated on air multiple times that I hoped he would run and that if he did, he would win. Later that evening on national television I declared that he would be the next president and IT WAS ON! I calmly explained to the panel of commentators that were holding back laughter that this was a man who had spent four decades building an international brand, was willing to self-fund his entire campaign and didn't give a damn if people were offended. Mr. Trump was in the business of branding, fighting and negotiating; the 2016 election was his race as far as I was concerned, everyone else was fighting to be in second place. I was immediately ridiculed and made the laughing stock of many networks; CNN invited me on their prime-time shows with five-versus-one panels to try to prove their biased opinions, badgering Mr. Trump from their ivory towers of both political parties. I never wavered, battling them back harder and harder each time.

But it did something that I didn't realize at the time. The "swamp" (backed by most of the media) as Mr. Trump named it, divided us into three parties rather than two: Democrats, Republicans and people like me who were just sick and tired of Washington as usual. The first shots of the new civil war were fired by the very people who were supposed to be representing us in the first place. And for what? To keep their own power because they saw a Trump presidency as a threat.

I can recall weekly occasions on Newsmax TV with Joe Concha and Rick Unger when Rick would yell at me, "He will never see above 5 percent" When it was 10, 15, and 25 percent, Rick would say "He'll never win the primary" or "No shot in the general." Every week he was wrong. Every time Mr. Trump would ignite a firestorm. I would have a dozen producers like Chad Wilkinson call me and ask if I was still on the Trump train. "More than ever," I would respond, knowing full well the panel I would face that evening. I can recall being laughed at by the major Fox hosts, and my almost-daily battles with Megyn Kelly that fed an even more ferocious level of support for Mr. Trump led to more requests by all networks. Though I was an unpaid surrogate of the campaign, I was moving the needle. The Republican National Committee, John McCain, Hillary Clinton surrogates, CNN, MSNBC and even some at Fox News fought a handful of us who threw down on behalf of the 45th president. Even Kelly Anne Conway and I, though friendly and cordial, would battle as she represented Ted Cruz.

My life was a rush: hitting the gym at 4:00 a.m., then the early morning and late evening news shows with eight-hour work days in between. At the time I was the operations director for a small media company run by a seemingly lunatic boss who was acted jealous of my public profile. In an effort not to get sued by him, (because that is the type of person he is), we'll call him "John". Though it was in my contract to allow me to continue my television appearances, he continually sought ways to stifle them, from assigning odd duties to eventually trying to force me to sign a document saying I wouldn't go on television anymore, changing the terms I was initially hired under. It was not the content of what I was saying, he actually agreed with almost every bit of it as he was a Trump supporter himself, it was that "John" was jealous of my public persona. He was in the same media arena but could not garner even remotely the same exposure. Things really came to a head at CPAC in 2016 when I was asked to introduce Mr. Trump, though he chose not to attend at the last minute.

While I knew this job was temporary, I maintained my support for Mr. Trump and worked to become a paid member of the campaign. In the spring of 2016 I was given a closed-door option to stop my television appearances or risk being fired. I asked "John" if he would like me to resign and how I would be compensated if I did due to our contractual agreement. I saw the writing on the wall and was going to force this company to fire me. A few weeks later while passing "John" in the hallway, he smiled, said hello and pulled into the main office where I was given a termination letter. The severance was quite fair, so I really don't hold a grudge.

Now, as a free agent, I asked the campaign to take me on as a permanent employee. Instead, I was scooped up by Eric Beach and Ed Rollins with the Great America PAC. This was Mr. Trump's largest and earliest independent super PAC. I was hired as the communication director and spokesman—a dream job for me. I was now getting paid full time to do exactly what I was doing for free for the last year. With 24/7 availability for the networks, I was doing two, three, four and oftentimes five hits a day on national networks. At that pace slips are inevitable, and I made a crack—that even I will admit was over the line—at the late John McCain after his feud with Mr. Trump over the "I like those who weren't captured" comment. Eric Beach chewed my ass but not without a good lesson learned. Compared to most people playing at this level, I was very green and was still learning.

It was a true shock to me how people were so irrational about their hatred for Mr. Trump. Having met the guy a few times by this point and having gotten to know both Donald Trump, Jr. and Eric Trump, I just could not compute what the problem was; they seemed great to me and even better for America. I can recall a CNN broadcast one night with a both Democrat and black panel that were unified in being pissed off about whatever their flavor of anger for Mr. Trump was that week. During the broadcast moderated by Don Lemon, one of the panelists made a personal remark that was overly patronizing and personally insulting. Thinking to myself that this dude is about 100 pounds lighter than me, he would NEVER say this to me on the street; my blood boiled, but I kept my cool. After the broadcast he made another snarky comment as we walked off the set; I turned to him and quietly said, "Disagree all you want with me but if you ever insult me like that again on national TV I will punch you in the throat." You should have seen him run; it became clear that this was our opposition. The opposition for Mr. Trump was incredible, irrational and uncontrolled hatred. This was the norm, though. Liberals and conservatives telling me that Mr. Trump would never win. These remarks only solidified my support even more, and we were creating a movement. I mention that moment in this book in full disclosure because I still had my mic on and I know some day somewhere if I run for office CNN will release that hot-mic moment, so I'll just get ahead of it.

Though I met a slew of great folks through this campaign, none were like the fellow Trump drum beaters of Brett, Rich and Rich's wife, Beth. Brett had even named his cat "Trump" back in the eighties. Rich and Brett were best friends from childhood and became independent successful businessmen; these guys embodied the American dream. We got them roped into the super PAC in a major way. They came to all of our events, they were huge supporters, and I took them to meet Mr. Trump one day in DC, too. In the weeks leading up to the election, we took their plane to Las Vegas for the last debate and toured multiple states with celebrities such as Rudy Giuliani, Katrina Pierson, Mike Huckabee, Sheriff David A. Clarke, Jr., John Voight and more—bouncing from two, three and sometimes four states in a single day. They were the best, constantly engaged doing anything they could to move the needle. If there were people on this planet who wanted Mr. Trump to win more than me, it was them.

During the last week before the election, Great America PAC launched our bus tour, hitting the key swing states. On November 7 we attended Mr. Trump's rally in North Carolina. Just before the rally, I met Mr. Trump in the hall backstage and he said "Carl, we are going to win big tomorrow." As I had from day one, I believed him. It was because I believed IN him even more so than believing what he espoused that I didn't care about the Access Hollywood tapes; as a matter of fact, I thought it was humanizing. I not only was fine with him breaking the presidential mold, I embraced it. I loved the guy and I knew the content of his character. Through all of the media clutter I saw a man that could have retired on a beach and lived a life of luxury, but chose to be ridiculed, to spend his personal fortune and to risk everything for a chance to save the country that gave him the opportunity to become who he was—and I admired that.

THE TRANSITION

We had won, and the cover of the *New York Post*—that I have proudly framed in my office—declared "Everyone was wrong." So began the transition. I was not an integral part of it, but I was very tied in to those who were. I was offered a "position" on the transition team; when I asked what I would be doing they said, "Well come down here and we will figure that out. Also its not paid and you need to cover all your own travel." Right. I explained, "I need to work to support my family and I can't just uproot for no pay or guarantee. Call me when you have a real job that needs to be done." As I stayed in touch with the teams leading the Department of Defense and US Department of State, I was assured a job in the DOD and even interviewed for Assistant Secretary of Defense for Public Affairs at the Pentagon. But it became apparent that there was an agenda different from the president's; none of the military folks who supported President Trump from the beginning were getting jobs, and if they were the jobs were low level. It was party insiders and mega donors that were landing the jobs first. After eight months, dozens of trips down to DC on my own dime for meetings, and countless phone calls with the transition folks, Johnny DeStefano, Reince Priebus and others, there was no credible job offer. Finally, I sent this letter:

> Reince,
> I want you to read this to understand my frustration with this slow process and my personal story that I think may shock you.
>
> I know over the last few days we have had many conversations and I do sincerely appreciate your time but I wanted to lay out why I am at the end of my rope with this process of endless promises and meetings with no achievement on my behalf.
>
> As a Navy SEAL I live by loyalty and principal. From day one I was there. I went head to head with everyone and backed a man I believed in, Donald Trump. I fought for him unlike anyone else in the field. I staked everything, my reputation, many friendships and my current job. Three months into this campaign I was given an option, continue to support Donald Trump on TV or leave my job. I chose to support Trump.
>
> With no paycheck, while going through a divorce and messy custody battle for my daughter I spent every waking minute

either on TV, knocking on doors in my home state or making phone calls to solicit donations and support for an unknown candidate in a sea of 17+ very qualified seasoned politicians.
ALL WITHOUT PAY.

I all but begged the campaign to take me on in a paid capacity, they said no but listed me as an unpaid surrogate, I did not waiver and continued my pursuit of support relentlessly. After months of this, thousands of interviews, 3000 + doors knocked on and many thousands of personal phone calls, I was picked up by Great America PAC. I was their spokesman and communications director where I worked 16+ hours a day 7 days a week in almost 30 states. I endured thousands more interviews, with unwavering support even on Trump's most controversial instances, and still did not waiver. During the campaign I never asked for anything nor did I expect anything. I did it because I believe in Trump and love my country.

On election night, I stood there till 3 in the morning until the race was called in his favor, as he walked down the stairs he saw the tears streaming down my face, shot me thumbs up and said thank you. Short of my childrens' birth, It was the proudest moment of my life as I knew we had elected a man who was truly going to Make America Great Again.

I never aspired to be nor asked for a position in the administration, I wanted to work in the private sector but was asked by many people, some very close to the president-elect to consider taking a job with the admin. Again ending the campaign ended my employment with the Great America PAC. I was offered two well paying jobs at communications firms but at the same time had been encouraged to pursue a job for the President. I was initially told that I "would be perfect for the

DoD", and even assured that I was a "shu-in" for the pentagon spokesman. After being sent down to the DoD 4 times for interviews that amounted to nothing, I was told by the White House to pursue other avenues due to a "friendly tug-o-war with the pentagon". I was instructed that there was going to be a shake up and to be patient and would be an excellent candidate for something in the White House. At the time, I was offered another job that I again passed on due to an assurance that I was going into the administration from your team, still nothing transpired.

Since my trip to the White House to visit you where I was assured "100%" in your words that there was a place for me, there has again been lots of activity but no results. Now 4 weeks later, I came back to DC, had had another "meeting" that amounted to nothing where they didn't even know what position I was there to discuss, only to be told that I "might get another meeting" in 2-3 weeks. I am not a wealthy man and have spent tens of thousands of dollars traveling to and from DC for useless meetings, put my life on hold with a newborn child and still defended EVERYTHING our President does, and this is how I have been treated.

Anyone who knows me always says "never bet against Carl" because I am a fighter, a doer, take pride in anything I do and never quit. I did not ask to join the administration, you guys asked me. I could do any job assigned better than any of the insiders and bureaucrats that are currently getting appointed before those of us that were there from the beginning. If it was not a good fit you should have told me from day one, and you know what? I would have still been loyal. I will always be loyal to President Trump, I would take a bullet for him. But I now understand that his agenda is hampered by you and other political insiders like you that *believe in structure over function and lack the conviction to see things through.*

So when you tell me to "hold on", "these things take time", and "be patient", after 8 months, bullshit. I put my life on hold, sacrificed more than you ever will know on the battlefield and now for the single man that I believe in more than my own father and you tell me that you can't get something done for me in over half a year??? What you lack is the political will to do it. keep in mind you would not be in the White House if it weren't for myself and a small handful of other people that were spit on, assaulted, ridiculed on national TV and made fun of by our own families for supporting someone that was told "can never win". I am at the end of my rope, does this administration want me or not, if so I need an answer by this Friday, if it can't happen by then I need to pursue another way to provide for my family.

In loyalty to the President,
Carl Higbie

Now in full disclosure, I like Reince Priebus on a personal level and believe that he is a good person. He always took my calls and responded to my emails, but the frustration I expressed here was that nothing was getting done. You see, Washington, DC is a bubble where activity constitutes achievement while actual achievement is secondary to name dropping and meetings that give the illusion of progress.

I found this out firsthand with my appointment that came shortly after that letter. I was appointed to the Chief of External Affairs for the Corporation for National and Community Service. What the hell is that? I had the same reaction. This was a small agency that soaked up a little more than a billion dollars of taxpayer money and appeared on the White House defund list. Having been in the nonprofit world, despite what CNN tells you about me, I am passionate about service to our country.

What you will only hear from me is that prior to accepting this job, I disclosed as much of the potential things I had in my past that could be an issue to both Reince Priebus and John DeStefano, as well as to Sean Doocey and Jennifer Locetta, staffers who processed appointments. I told them that I had been a very controversial person in the past and explicitly asked if any this was going to be an issue. All of my social media profiles were public domain, my books were all available and I offered to send them copies. I told them I was an open book and wanted to be as upfront as possible. The definitive answer was that I was cleared for duty.

In August of 2017 I took my desk in Washington as one of three senior appointees at the agency. We had a career bureaucrat as an acting CEO that had little interest in the president or his agenda that I viewed as a traffic cone in the middle of the road of efficiency. Her pet, the acting Chief of Staff, wasn't any better; he actually went out of his way to stifle progress. They were interested in the status quo; the less they could do on the taxpayers dime the better for them. We were awaiting a CEO to be confirmed by the Senate and were forced to deal with this unfortunate reality for the time being.

I attacked this job with all the vigor and passion you could imagine, remembering from my high school wrestling coach Brad to "never half ass anything, whole ass everything." I dug in, reviewing budgets, the chain of command, processes and procedures. My conclusion after just a few weeks: this place was a bureaucratic disaster, a shit show! Wasted money, redundancies and promotions to useless departments, instead of firings, were everywhere. I brought these up to my appointed counterparts, including our General Counsel, who told me not to worry about it. "Sit there for two years, put this on your résumé and let the career folks handle the work," he said. Is your head spinning? Mine was, so I got to work.

I slashed external contracts with companies that were being paid millions of dollars for services that, even upon request, I could not get results or specifics on. The lack of services being provided in exchange for the millions of dollars screamed kickbacks and cronyism, though I have no proof of that. I garnered more results from free Google alerts, including $200,000 to $300,000 spent on fifty-second videos. I discovered that social media ad buys returned such a low rate of viewership that we were paying almost a dollar per view on certain posts and that hundreds of thousands of dollars were spent to design and print materials that didn't appear to exist—I could not find them anywhere in the office or at the field sites they were allegedly sent to. What the hell was going on? No one seemed to care. I was actually told to stop obsessing over it! As I dug deeper, I found that this government agency under President Trump was granting funds and resources to programs in California that helped illegal immigrants get jobs and housing and was providing services through our VISTA program to the CAIR (Center for American Islamic Relations) Minnesota chapter whose leader bashed the president. I found many more shocking allocations of taxpayer dollars. There were departments that were middlemen to middlemen and liaisons to liaisons; I spent more time figuring out who to talk to than actually getting things done. Structure trumped function and there was almost no function. Every site, grantee or program I visited made an effort to complain about how inefficient the DC office was. Don't believe me? Feel free to make a Freedom of Information Act request; all of my emails are also public record for seven years. The crazy part was that I was the only appointee that was willing to raise hell about it; everyone else seemed content, at least initially. This was not what the president saw fit to put me here for, so I was going to change things.

I took most of our services in house, giving raises to people who actually worked hard and forcing those that didn't to actually come to work and return a damn email. I traveled around the country to dozens of states on a listening tour, shooting video and finding out how we as the centralized agency could better serve our communities and grantees. All this was met with severe opposition from most of the career staff in DC, many of whom didn't want to change or even work. Some got on board but were hesitant to be too vocal for fear of their own job.

What did I get in return? I asked the agency's human resources team to do a survey of my department due to incompetence of my deputy, Marc Young. This is the guy who literally didn't give me a message left by the vice president's office for a whole week, and it would have been longer if I didn't ask him. So, human resources did the survey and it was clear that they were willing to say anything to get me to go. The survey alleged anything from sexual comments to creating a hostile work environment. As a Navy SEAL, I strongly suggested that they reconsider their understanding of a "hostile" work environment. But this was what I was working with. Upon receipt of this ridiculous review, the majority of my staff formed a line outside the HR door to protest their findings; they all wanted to voice their concerns that the report was not what most people expressed in their interviews and that my immediate employees actually liked working for me.

The career staff wanted me gone, and half a year later a story aired from a series of 2012-2013 radio shows I had done after returning from war. I had to resign, or the president would be left to answer questions for the next six months. But what did I say? While many were harsh, some even racially insensitive and rude, they were not what the headlines portrayed. Many were portrayed grossly out of context and all were said in an effort to garner attention as a shock jock radio host like Howard Stern. I'll admit it was not done elegantly, but it was not out of hate; it was out of concern for issues phrased in a way for shock and awe to garner ratings. Never in a million years did I ever think I would have been a presidential appointee.

Following my resignation, I had time to reflect on my statements from five years ago at the time and on the impact on my family, friends and even our culture. While I regret some, stand by some, and apologized for those that were out of line, many comments were weaponized not necessarily against me but to harm our president via the left's increasing obsession with identity politics. I know this because these interviews had surfaced before when I ran for Congress and no one seemed to care; but they did when they could attach it to President Trump. While some reporters pat themselves on the back as "the free press holding people accountable," some are not as interested in a *fair* press as we have seen with the Roseanne Barr-Samantha Bee controversy.

In full disclosure, the author of CNN's piece did reach out for comment a few hours before publication, but I was instructed not to respond by the White House. After my resignation, however, not one CNN show was willing to host me to debate the issue after the article came out. They ran dozens of segments on me, content with a one-sided assassination without context or even an interest in my input. Keeping suit, the liberal media was more interested in assassinating me over less than two minutes of my past rather than discussing the whole content of the comments in question.

Despite reaching out to producers I knew and had worked with during the campaign, none returned my emails or calls. The only person who contacted me from CNN was Don Lemon with whom, off camera, I have a good relationship. While he was disappointed and even hurt by some of my comments, he knew that was not who I was at heart. He heard me out because he wanted the whole story; none of that was ever aired, however.

This political landscape is becoming increasingly dangerous for anyone who challenges the far left's progressive agenda. Allies of

President Trump and even our families are accused of things ranging from sexual assault to bigotry and are shouted down and ridiculed for views different from their own (ironically, the definition of bigotry), but they tolerate and even thrive on the vial response from their following. Case in point: Sarah Huckabee was shouted out of a restaurant for her support of President Trump while the *New York Times* hired a devout self-admitted racist with hundreds of tweets about white people. I have received hate mail, vile comments about my family and friends and even death threats. These come from the same people that preach tolerance for all views; the irony is almost overwhelming.

So, what is the solution for a society that is almost evenly divided between two starkly different viewpoints? With the evolution of internet, social media and mass information distribution, facts are often subjected to the views of those with the biggest microphone. National media markets are based primarily out of New York and Washington, DC; viewing the electoral map with roughly a 97% geographic win for President Trump, local constituencies are not evenly represented. The national media report what they want, nothing they don't want and, in my case, are not interested in a debate.

The irony is that at the time of publication, I am involved with the Urban Revitalization Coalition that is run by the same people as the National Diversity Coalition. In my previous role that I stepped down from, I was literally the face for national community service, working to make it more efficient than ever before. A week before the story surfaced in 2017, I was reading books to minority children in Los Angeles who were not even born when these statements were said. Before that, I was helping veterans overcome opioid addictions in Colorado and Montana, handing out Christmas presents to low-income families all over New England, helping senior citizens get engaged in Neighborhood Watch programs and many other initia-tives. During high school I spent two summers on mission trips to

Central America developing a program for orphaned children in predominantly minority communities to be paired with a big brother or big sister program.

Had the media reported facts rather than an agenda, their headlines may have been different. After my resignation, dozens of people from the DC office and programs I had visited reached out to express how upset they were to no longer be working with me. Do we live in the past or present? What speaks louder, words or actions? Had I not written this book, you would never know that. Who else could I have helped? But was the left interested in that? No. They wanted to hurt President Trump and I was a vehicle for that. The culture war the left wages is actually against the very people the left screams are so in need and should be helped; these were the exact people that I was serving, and the left didn't care.

Liberals have ratcheted up the personalized destruction tied to identity politics and I, for one, am sick of it. The left screams for civility yet calls anyone who doesn't agree with their radical views a Nazi, bigot, xenophobe or any variation of ist, phobe or the like. If they really want a solution, they need to drop the manufactured moral outrage and actually try to be civil to conservatives. I want civility, I want debate and I want a unified country, but not at the expense of laying down, surrendering my principals and being trampled on. When you are insulted, don't walk away, speak up and engage the debate politely; when you are threatened, stand your ground without aggression. When you are assaulted by the lawless liberal mobs of Antifa and their ilk, defend yourself at any cost, do not retreat. When the left realizes that they can't walk all over us, then we can have civility. People will use this paragraph against me as inciting violence; those that do are fools. I am aiming for peace at all costs but do not confuse that with my commitment to stand my ground. When the left stops the attacks, I am open to working with them. That is the Crisis of Culture, and so I wrote this book.

PART ONE

BATTLEGROUNDS

WHERE DO YOU STAND ON
IDEOLOGICAL FRONTS?

"If you're not a liberal at twenty you have no heart, if you're not a conservative at forty you have no brain."

SIR WINSTON CHURCHILL

MORE THAN EVER THERE is a struggle between liberals and conservatives on the national political battlefield. Unfortunately, this war is being fought between one group of Americans and another, instead of all Americans coming together to stand up against those who seek to divide. This is driven by a party that relishes division so that they can be viewed as the mortar between those divided groups, but the real aim is to divide and conquer.

The definitions of these two camps are relatively simple. People often make decisions, from jobs to how to raise their children to how to vote, based on political ideology. The parties are changing, however, and there are a growing number in our society that don't truly understand where they fall in modern political affiliation and may vote based on issues they later regret, for example, those who voted for Barrack Obama based on charisma and smooth talking points. There is no doubt that he will probably go down in history as the greatest politician in my lifetime; his policies were horrible, but man did he sell it. Had Americans done their homework and knew the historical failures that President Obama's proposed policies were based on, most people might have voted differently and perhaps many things would have been better. In order to vote in our best interest, we must educate ourselves lest we end up with another Barrack Obama in our lifetimes. Many of these issues will make you question whether you vote with your brain or your heart. This chapter will discuss how the propaganda game is played and intent versus their actions. It will also help you understand where you are now and where you stand.

Even as a modern conservative, my views don't always agree with either party and exist in a grey zone—and it was people in this grey zone that President Trump was able to capture. As you examine the issues below, you may see that you do not fit into either party. I propose civil compromise, not necessarily based on my view, but based on what is best for America.

LIBERAL (DEMOCRAT)

The liberal left believes in government action to achieve equality through economic and social oversight. They view themselves and their policies as the great equalizer. If you earn more it is your duty to repay society. Liberals believe that it is the duty of the government to alleviate social ills and to protect civil liberties and individual and human rights. Competition is unhealthy, and everyone should receive a trophy for effort rather than achievement. They believe the role of the government should be to guarantee that no one is in need. Liberal policies generally emphasize that big government is the answer. If they don't like something they ban it, and if they can't ban it they regulate and tax it because the government will always ensure a fair and equitable society.

Conservative (Republican)

The conservative right believes in personal responsibility, limited government, free markets, individual liberty, traditional American values, a strong national defense and pride in our country's success. They believe that you reap what you sow; the harder you work the more you prosper and vice versa. They believe the role of government should be to provide people the freedom and security necessary to pursue their own goals. Conservative policies generally emphasize empowerment of the individual.

Generally, a liberal believes in big government; a conservative believes in limited government. Conservatives stand on the facts and data of their policies while liberals will dismiss facts and turn to emotion in order to promote theirs. I once published an op-ed that I feel best illustrates the issue where I questioned the Democratic platform:

> With the midterms creeping up on us, the political line between left and right has never been clearer and more divisive. With new leaders of the Democratic party emerging like Alexandria Ocasio-Cortez, leading campaigns to sell far left policies deeply rooted in historical failure to their base versus and Republicans running on the success of President Trump, my prediction is a landslide for Republicans in the house. Despite what the media covers, the success of this administration cannot be denied. So why would everyone not get behind at least the good things the President is doing? Begging the question, what do Democrats actually stand for? Many of the

5

policies they promote on the Democrat's party homepage are literally what Donald Trump has either proposed or even accomplished; "Raising worker's wages", "Infrastructure", "Fostering a manufacturing renaissance", "Promoting trade that is fair and benefits the American worker" but if you hear democrats campaign, they resist all of the President's efforts to accomplish anything. They campaign for; wealth redistribution, State controlled "free" health care, open boarders, a foreign policy of appeasement, and of course resisting the President.

"God never intended for one group of people to live in superfluous inordinate wealth while others live in abject deadening poverty."

NANCY PELOSI

This statement is ironic coming from someone whose net worth exceeds $100 million; nevertheless, wealth redistribution is a key platform of the Democratic Party. Historically known as communism or socialism, wealth redistribution has never worked. Nazi stands for National Socialist German Workers' Party and we had a world war against it barely sixty years ago; people were thrown in jail for the mere allegation of an affiliation with communism. Two decades later, America was almost willing to wage a nuclear war against Russia to prevent communism from spreading. Yet in 2016, a legitimate contender for the Democratic presidential nomination ran as a socialist. The left is pushing for economic policies that have destroyed every nation that embraced those policies. The ideals and principles of socialism have been resurrected by the left, renamed to progressivism and wrapped in shinny promises of "free stuff." If these policies actually worked, why are liberal utopias crime ridden and deep in debt?

"We will start by reducing (health care) premiums by as much as $2500 per family per year."

PRESIDENT BARACK OBAMA

State-controlled health care, also known as socialized medicine, was not only President Obama's signature legislation and his greatest failure, but it produced a net negative gain for the average American's health care. Obamacare expanded the overburdened Medicare system, jacked up the cost of health insurance by more than 100 percent in some states, and did almost nothing to address the cost of healthcare services. Many districts were left with little or even no choice on the exchanges, the promise of keeping your plan or doctor went up in smoke and the big hand of government forced people to purchase a private product that was, in most cases, inferior to what they already had. Years after the individual mandate was repealed, Democrats continue to hang on to a socialized health care plan that already failed the American people.

"My dream is a hemispheric common market, with open trade and open borders sometime in the future..."

HILLARY CLINTON

Open borders and amnesty, another Democratic Party platform, do not put America first. This policy is championed by those who are less concerned with the well-being of our own citizens and the security of our nation than illegal immigrants. Republicans and President Trump are not anti-immigrant, we simply want to know who is coming here and why. Such reasonable logic could have prevented the murder of Kate Steinle among many others. We also wish not to reward those who broke the law with citizenship ahead of those who came here legally. For Democrats, this is selfishly about votes—they think that if they grant citizenship to more than twelve million people "on behalf of humanity" those people will vote loyally democratic, and they might. But to think that the Democratic Party is doing this in the interest of humanity is preposterous; this is about maintaining power.

"If you want to negotiate with (North Korean leader) Kim Jong Un, and your goal is to avoid war and try to be able to have a diplomatic resolution, the worst thing you can do is first threaten to destroy his country in the United Nations."

JOHN KERRY

Months later after President Trump's continued pressure, leaders of North and South Korea met to end the multigenerational Korean war and Kim Jong Un agreed to denuclearize. The foreign policy of the progressive left is nothing short of appeasement and lowers our standing on the world stage. President Obama's non-interventionalist policies gave pallets of cash to Iran, bowed to foreign leaders and went on a global apology tour. Did it work? No, it was a dismal failure resulting in the creation of ISIS, North Korea's increased hostility, debilitating cuts to our military and other threats to America. Much like immigration, Democrats put the desires of other countries, even those that don't like America, in front of our own interests.

"I will go and take Trump out tonight."

MAXINE WATERS

The only actionable statement of policy from the Democratic Party since President Trump was elected has been to resist his agenda. If you go to the Democratic Party platform page, the first thing on their priorities list is "Raising Workers' Wages." President Trump has done that, so why do they fight him on literally everything? It doesn't matter what issue, no matter if they voted for it in the last cycle or in the last decade, if President Trump stands for it they're are against it, even at the detriment of America.

This quintet of issues is the Democratic platform. Anyone who opposes these views have been labeled foolish, heartless, racist or any corresponding variant. We are in an ideological war between one party that is diving headfirst into the policies of historical blunders and another party that supports the policies that made us the greatest nation in history. It is truly frightening that after all this, our elections remain a 50/50 proposition.

It's important to explore the current battlegrounds upon which daily political wars are fought. The left preys on people who feel they don't belong 100 percent to the Republican Party. Social deviation does not exempt you from the Republican Party as the old guard will tell you. This is where traditional Republicans have failed the public relations war... until now. Enter the 2016 elections when one party stood for the new direction of social and liberal economic policies while the other stood for what seemed to make the most sense, no matter how offensive it was, and the American people elected the latter. That is why it is important to learn about the issues in order to make educated decisions. So what are the issues? Tally your answers to see where you stand; if you are like me, there may be issues for which you don't fall into either category. Let's start with the most controversial, even among the political parties.

ABORTION

"I've noticed everybody that is for abortion has already been born."

PRESIDENT RONALD REAGAN

"One method of destroying a concept is by diluting its meaning. Observe that by ascribing rights to the unborn, i.e., the nonliving, the anti-abortionists obliterate the rights of the living."

AYN RAND

"(T)he line between lawful and unlawful abortion will be marked by the fact of having sensation and being alive."

ARISTOTLE

LIBERAL

A fetus is not a human life, it is a part of a woman's body, so it does not have separate individual rights. A woman has the right to decide what happens with her body. The government should provide taxpayer-funded abortions for women who cannot afford them. The decision to have an abortion is a personal choice of a woman regarding her own body, and the federal government must protect and even subsidize this right. Women have the right to affordable, safe and legal abortions, including partial birth abortion.

CONSERVATIVE

Human life begins at conception; therefore, abortion is murder. An unborn baby, as a living being, has rights separate from those of the mother. Conservatives oppose taxpayer-funded abortion because taxpayers should not have to foot the bill for something that is not a right and is against their beliefs.

The pro-choice, pro-life argument is one of the defining distinctions between liberals and conservatives. The pro-choice, pro-life argument can make a person who fundamentally agrees with everything else from the other party still vote against it. Conservatives fight for the rights of an unborn child, and the liberals push for those rights to be given to the mother, with help from the government when the mother can't afford to have that so-called right. This debate often centers on the ethical questions of who the government must protect, the rights of those who cannot defend themselves and, in essence, when life begins. The irony is that despite *Roe v. Wade*[1], if you murder a pregnant woman at any stage, you are eligible to be charged with double homicide. If NASA discovers a single organism in a block of ice on another planet, that is considered "life."

I do not wish to answer these questions, especially the latter, but rather I offer a political solution to solve the political fracture. While I think that abortion is morally wrong, I also believe that the federal government should leave the issue to be decided by each state per the Tenth Amendment.

SOLUTION

Since we will probably not overturn *Roe v. Wade,* our generation should work to have the federal government allow abortion as it is now but ban abortion after a certain stage (perhaps after viability) while not funding abortion on any level. If the left wants it, they can rally support from their base, or, God forbid, pay for it themselves.

The solution is simple, yet it offers a fair compromise. If you don't like it, don't do it and your tax dollars won't fund it. If you want an abortion and your state has decided it is legal, do it. The federal government needs to get out of the way and allow morality and states' rights to fill the vacuum. To some people, abortion is a lifeline, an out for a future that they are not prepared to undertake. For others, it is an abomination, murder and morally wrong.

For those who are pro-life: demonstrate, protest and reach out to those who may get abortions and dissuade them. In short, seek not a political route to cure what you believe is an evil, but rather use a public relations campaign or religious outreach program. You do not need the federal government telling you what to do with an unborn child just as you do not need the federal government telling you what firearms you can and cannot own.

For those who are pro-choice: make up for the loss of government funding by seeking private donations from your "fat cats" like Michael Moore (no pun intended) and George Soros to fund your abortion clinics and Planned Parenthood rather than coordinating protests with women dressed as vaginas. If the government does not fund abortion, this does not mean an end to abortion or women's health care.

AFFIRMATIVE ACTION

"Affirmative action has a negative effect on our society when it means counting us like so many beans and dividing us into separate piles."

JOHN KASICH, GOVERNOR OF OHIO AND
2016 PRESIDENTIAL CANDIDATE

"Affirmative action was never meant to be permanent, and now is truly the time to move on to some other approach."

SUSAN ESTRICH, ATTORNEY AND LIBERAL
ACTIVIST

"If you don't like affirmative action, what is your plan to guarantee a level playing field of opportunity?"

MAYNARD JACKSON, DEMOCRAT AND
FIRST BLACK MAYOR OF ATLANTA

Don't worry Mayor Jackson, like always, I have a plan.

LIBERAL

Because of past racism, liberals believe minorities were, and still are. deprived of the same education and employment opportunities as whites. The government must give minorities a leg up—provide a "level playing field"—to compensate for this perceived disadvantage. They believe that America is still a racist society and that federal affirmative action legislation is necessary to cure this ill. Minorities still lag behind whites in all statistical measurements of success because society keeps them down.[2]

CONSERVATIVE

Individuals should be admitted to schools and hired for jobs based on their ability. It is unfair to use race as a factor in the selection process. Reverse discrimination is not a solution for racism. Some individuals in society are racist, but American society as a whole is not. Preferential treatment of certain races *is* racism, and it is actually very offensive to minorities to suggest that they are not as able as white people to achieve success based on their own skills and not their skin color.

First, let me make cracks where due. Thanks go to President Lyndon B. Johnson for the War on Poverty and Great Society. He neither won the war nor created anything close to a "great society," but that was really never his intention. This was made evident when he was alleged to have said (to be clear this is what LBJ said, not me), "These Negroes, they're getting pretty uppity these days and that's a problem for us since they've got something now they never had before, the political pull to back up their uppityness. Now we've got to do something about this, we've got to give them a little something, just enough to quiet them down, not enough to make a difference."[3]

He was also alleged to have said, "I'll have those niggers voting Democratic for the next 200 years[4]," referring to those same government welfare programs that he boasted would make our country great. The affirmative action issue is constantly perceived as something supported by the left because they want to lift minorities up and is boycotted on the right because they want to hold minorities down. It's also often thought that these policies are needed because America is a racist country because of slavery. Well, quick history lesson: slavery has been carried out for thousands of years in hundreds of countries, territories and empires, and is not unique to America. What does make America unique is that we are the first nation ever to fight a war among the ruling race or group to free the enslaved. I would call us the least racist country ever. Mind you, this was all led by the first Republican president: Abraham Lincoln.

Second, affirmative action *is* racism because it penalizes one race and rewards another simply on race rather than merit. This is the very definition of racism because it is nothing less than unfair treatment based on skin color and ethnicity. These programs degrade society because the best person for the job is not necessarily given the job. For example, would you want a second-rate firefighter, who got the job just because his skin as a different color, to save your children from a burning building? This instance happened in Connecticut, which subsequently ceased the policy following a lawsuit. Affirmative action creates artificial rewards for being a member of a particular group. In a fair and just society, jobs, positions, scholarships and other life prizes should be awarded on the sole basis of merit.

Further, affirmative action harms minorities and is very degrading. Affirmative action policies tell minorities that "you are not capable or talented enough to achieve anything on your own, so we will help you." Even if the minority achieves a goal or success, he or she will always be looked upon with a question of whether his or her gains in life were really earned. Think this is a little harsh? That is the reality of this imposed policy regardless of your feelings.

If we would simply allow the free market to work and have a true meritocracy to be reborn in America, we would all be better off. Let's do what our founders did: if you want something work for it, no matter the odds. Competition is what breeds innovation and ultimately our nation's dominance. Hire the right person for the right job, not someone based on skin tone. Is it fair to the American people to not have the best policeman just to fill a diversity quota? What about a surgeon or an attorney? No, it is not fair to anyone and the unintended consequences can be catastrophic. Neither the recipient of the policy nor the ultimate person who receives the goods or service provided by the hire is served. Racism of any form is bad for our citizens, our economy and our nation as a whole.

Solution

The best man or woman gets the job, period. Our society and institutions should not tolerate racism in any form; however, it is an individual's right to show distaste to anyone regardless of race, religion or creed. Get the government out of our lives and far away from our businesses and allow meritocracy to flourish. If any preferential treatment should occur (to answer Mayor Jackson's musing), offer the preferential treatment on a means-test basis.

THE DEATH PENALTY

"A humane and generous concern for every individual, his health and his fulfillment, will do more to soothe the savage heart than the fear of state-inflicted death, which chiefly serves to remind us how close we remain to the jungle."

RAMSEY CLARK, NEW YORK TIMES

"How come life in prison doesn't mean life? Until it does, we're not ready to do away with the death penalty. Stop thinking in terms of "punishment" for a minute and think in terms of safeguarding innocent people from incorrigible murderers."

JESSE VENTURA, FORMER GOVERNOR OF
MINNESOTA AND NAVY SEAL

LIBERAL

The death penalty should be abolished. It is inhumane and "cruel and unusual" punishment. Imprisonment and rehabilitation are the appropriate courses of action for murder. Every execution includes the risk of killing an innocent person.

CONSERVATIVE

The death penalty fits the crime of murder and, if carried out properly, is neither "cruel" nor "unusual." Executing a murderer is the appropriate punishment for taking an innocent life. The death penalty provides closure to victims' families, deters other would-be-criminals and provides retribution against the wrongdoer. Additionally, the death penalty is part of the historic American criminal justice system and widely accepted by our culture.

. . .

I support the death penalty. What I struggle with is the neutrality of those making the decision. One argument often heard against the death penalty is that of racial inequality. In 2012, for example, blacks constituted 34 percent of all death penalty executions[5] yet blacks only constitute roughly 13 percent of the American population. Could this be because we are a racist society, or is this because black people statistically commit and are convicted of more homicides? Given pure statistics, I lean toward the latter. Many first and second-degree murders relate to the illegal drug trade in inner cities where there are higher concentrations of minorities. Could this skew the statistics? I will leave that to the reader to decide.

An argument in favor of the death penalty is to save the American taxpayer the cost of incarceration. This, too, is a losing argument, as the death penalty generally costs more than incarceration. Don't believe it? Look at these facts: in Texas the average cost of a death penalty sentence with litigation and accommodation is $2.3 million, which is roughly three times the amount it costs the state to house a prisoner for forty years at the highest cost-level of security.[6] Clearly, the economical solution is to champion life in prison rather than death, right?

The question then becomes the societal and moral impact of the death penalty. For many, the death penalty is necessary to provide justice and also closure for victims and their families. Some crimes are just too horrible to allow the perpetrators to live a long life in prison. Therefore, I am happy to have my tax dollars pay to eliminate criminals even at a higher cost than incarceration. Death must always be an option for the most horrendous crimes because some crimes dictate a punishment no less.

It is understandable, and I sympathize, that someone would be hesitant to trust the same institutions that run the Department of Motor Vehicles (DMV) to make life and death decisions, but when it comes to justice that is one area where the US Constitution explicitly allows the federal government to intervene. So there is a convincing constitutional argument for the cost of death penalties being a reasonable cost for taxpayers.

Solution

Under the Tenth Amendment the states should be able to determine the issue and have a criminal justice system that reflects the values of their citizens. I can only hope that the states will support the death penalty, as I believe that such a punishment is the only just punishment in some cases.

THE ECONOMY

"Government's view of the economy could be summed up in a few short phrases: If it moves, tax it. If it keeps moving, regulate it. And if it stops moving, subsidize it."

PRESIDENT RONALD REAGAN

"Look, if you've been successful, you didn't get there on your own...If you've got a business, you didn't build that. Somebody else made that happen."

PRESIDENT BARRACK OBAMA

LIBERAL

A market system where the government regulates the economy is best because the government is not corruptible and knows best how to manage an economy. Government must protect citizens from the greed of big business and, unlike the private sector, the government is motivated by public interest. Government regulation in all areas of the economy is necessary so no one makes "too much" money and everyone can get a fair shot. There should be redistribution of wealth on some level because the rich should pay their fair share. No matter one's success, government and society had a hand in one's achievement and should redistribute one's wealth. Government can create wealth and its spending leads to economic prosperity.

CONSERVATIVE

Free markets, competition, capitalism and private sector innovation create the greatest opportunity and the highest potential for anyone willing to work and produce. One is rewarded for his or her contribution to the economy. What one earns, one should keep, except for *reasonable* taxes. Free markets produce economic growth, create jobs and lead to higher standards of living for everyone. The government does not create wealth, but rather confiscates it. Excessive taxes and regulations burden the private sector.

The bedrock principle of liberalism is the belief that money is not the property of he who earns it, but the amount of profit the government allows one to keep. Conservatives believe that money belongs to those who earn it and taxes, therefore, are a tolerated form of wealth confiscation.

Enter the Trump tax cut. President Trump passed the first major tax reform since President Reagan. Can you guess what happened? Even the possibility of tax reform rocketed the stock market, adding $7 trillion to the nation's economy in his first year as president. Once passed, major corporations handed out bonuses and increased pay along with expansion here in America, not because of government intervention, but because of reduced government regulation. Eighteen months into the Trump presidency, gross domestic production hit 4.1%, a number we were told would likely never happen. And not a single Democrat voted for the policies that led us there.

Liberals lack the understanding that business owners, not government, create real jobs in our economy; government salaries are paid through the confiscated wealth of private earnings. If the left seeks private sector job creation and government revenue, then they should get the government's heavy foot off the throat of business leaders and allow them to breathe the fresh air of liberty. That heavy foot is crushing the windpipe of American business with regulation and taxes, suffocating our economy. The Trump administration's sweeping repeal of regulation should be a testament to this.

For example, I owned a very successful tree service and lumber business in Virginia Beach. Like many small businesses, I often struggled to meet many of the oppressive regulations and standards demanded by our government. Occasionally—not in defiance but in lack of notice, understanding or knowledge of regulation—the government fined the business for small violations of those complex regulations. I faced additional penalties in the form of taxes: taxes on income, taxes to pay part of an employee's social security and, with Obamacare, an obligation to pay employees' health care insurance or pay an additional fine. There is no doubt that the government impeded my business's bottom line. With money saved from tax cuts or from fines, I would not have hoarded the profits—as leftists would suggest—but rather I would have reinvested my profit in other business ventures, thus creating more jobs.

My experience is common; many small business owners across our nation echo this sentiment. How many jobs has our economy lost through punitive taxation and bloated government regulation? How many jobs have been created since President Trump eased regulations and tax burdens? These are fact-based realities, not opinion. It is incumbent upon our generation to reduce the role of government in business, thereby allowing the private sector—especially small businesses—to thrive.

SOLUTION

It's simple: reduce government spending, taxes and regulations as President Trump has done. Our government must continue reining in these things because the more our country is in debt, the more taxes we will need to pay, and this is a direct violation of our freedoms.

ENERGY

"Drill baby drill."

SARAH PALIN, VICE PRESIDENTIAL
CANDIDATE AND GOVERNOR OF ALASKA

"However many jobs might be generated by a Keystone pipeline... they're going to be a lot fewer than the jobs that are created by extending the payroll tax cut and extending unemployment insurance."

PRESIDENT BARACK OBAMA

LIBERAL

Fossil fuels harm the environment and are an unsustainable form of energy. America must adopt alternative energy. The government should subsidize alternative energy and increase taxes on conventional energy sources to entice people to "go green." Tax dollars should fund increased exploration of alternative energy sources such as wind and solar power because these sources of energy are not currently economically viable. The government must increase regulations on the gas, oil and coal industries because these industries pollute the land and prevent America from finding alternatives to their "dirty" energy.

CONSERVATIVE

If we got it, let's use it. Oil, gas and coal are our current primary sources of energy and are overly abundant in the US. New drilling and fracking techniques would increase our production if only we could get government regulations out of the way. Increased domestic production creates lower prices and less dependence on foreign oil. It has become scientifically and economically obvious that wind and solar power will not provide plentiful, affordable sources of power anytime soon. While fossil fuels are in fact a limited resource and will one day need to be replaced, we need to increase domestic energy production until alternative energy is truly a viable option. Domestic energy production will increase our national sovereignty, as we will not be beholden to other energy-rich nations. Further, we will lower the cost of energy while creating jobs and lessening the financial burden on American citizens.

In 2012 oil companies profited roughly 8.3 cents on every gallon of oil sold. The federal government alone netted roughly 13 cents on each gallon; this does not include state and local taxes on that same gallon. Why is the government making nearly double what the producer is? It does not make sense and neither does our nation's policy on energy production. Liberals seek to regulate and tax the industry, an industry vital to our nation's economic prosperity. If unburdened from some regulatory hindrances, for example drilling offshore, the industry would flourish and make us less dependent on foreign oil, in addition to the opportunity for our economy to prosper and expand with the price of growth (essentially fuel) lower. Yet the left fails to see the clear choice for a better future.

With our 2016 energy deficit of more than nine million barrels of oil per day, about one and a half times as much as we produce,[7] it is clear that we need more domestic production of traditional energy sources. The left, however, is insistent on solar energy and wind farms. These industries are neither economically viable nor have the ability to meet our needs.

SOLUTION

Continue President Trump's reduction of regulations and allow more energy exploration in the United States. Currently, it is impossible for this nation to survive without petroleum products. With new techniques, such as fracking, the gas industry could flourish. We should promote the development of natural gas exploration and drilling while easing the burdens on the oil industry. Our generation should encourage the government to reduce the red tape and allow the free market to meet America's needs. While there will be an initial outcry, like there was on the Keystone Pipeline, those critics will soon be silenced with cheaper prices at the pump.

Let's be clear: I am not opposed to the government taxing our fuel for revenue, as long as the government does so appropriately. However, taxes that dwarf the oil companies' profit is punitive. Additionally, our generation must reduce regulations to encourage growth and development. The left should perceive this as a win-win as they get to tax an industry and regulate it. We only ask that they reduce both.

Unleash the private sector. My bet is that if President Trump were to say, "The first American company to develop a clean, renewable, reliable energy source comparable or greater to fossil fuel will pay no payroll, corporate or employee personal taxes for ten years," you would have the next industrial revolution through innovation. As Americans, we could deliver that solution in less than three years because of the *lack* of government intervention.

GLOBAL WARMING & CLIMATE CHANGE

"Global warming -- at least the modern nightmare vision -- is a myth. I am sure of it and so are a growing number of scientists. But what is really worrying is that the world's politicians and policy makers are not."

DAVID BELLAMY, BRITISH AUTHOR, BROADCASTER, ENVIRONMENTAL CAMPAIGNER AND BOTANIST

"All across the world, in every kind of environment and region known to man, increasingly dangerous weather patterns and devastating storms are abruptly putting an end to the long-running debate over whether or not climate change is real. Not only is it real, it's here, and its effects are giving rise to a frighteningly new global phenomenon: the man-made natural disaster."

PRESIDENT BARACK OBAMA

Liberal

There is "undeniable evidence" of global warming caused by an increased production of carbon dioxide due to the burning of fossil fuels (coal, oil and natural gas). The US is a major contributor to global warming because it consumes a large percentage of the world's fossil fuels. We need laws and more regulations to reduce carbon emissions in the United States, and we must act immediately to save the planet. Some in Congress state that "97% of scientists agree mankind contributes to global warming."[8]

CONSERVATIVE

Our planet is a ball of rock spinning over 1,000 miles per hour, suspended in a vacuum with 300-degree temperature fluctuations, orbiting 93 million miles from our nearest heat source... temperature fluctuations are inevitable, mankind's presence must have *some* effect, but contributions are marginal. Change in global temperature is therefore natural and occurs over long periods of time. Science has not demonstrated conclusively that humans can affect permanent change to the earth's temperature. Proposed laws to reduce carbon emissions are not economically comparable to the effect on the environment and will cause significant price increases for fuel, food and consumer products. More government regulations in an attempt to stop global warming will only send more Americans into economic hardship. Many reputable scientists support this theory with facts.

I find it highly ironic that the left expects conservatives to accept this as settled science while refusing to award the same respect to gender identification, but I digress. As a young student, the public school system required me to read the Weekly Reader, a liberal publication for elementary students. One article I vividly recall was on climate change. The left, even then, was using climate change as a political tool. The article reported that man's use of fossil fuels, manufactured products, specifically CFC's from private and commercial use, and our general way of life was causing the world to experience wild changes in temperature.

By politicizing climate change, the left has accomplished two things.

First, any change in the climate, no matter the actual cause, benefits them because they can cite man's activity as the cause. Second, they have a manufactured crisis they can manipulate to push through legislation and government control, thus expanding the role of government in our lives.[9] Frankly, the left has played the global warming card perfectly. The Republicans have allowed the left to frame the argument, indoctrinate the public, especially the youth, and use the issue to promulgate regulations and more so, control. If one disagrees with these regulations, he or she either foolishly disregards the "undeniable evidence" or worse yet, does not care about the planet.

When you take into account how much Al Gore's and Leonardo DiCaprio's multimillion-dollar mansions and use of private jets contribute to their personal carbon footprint in the world, it is obvious to see that the left only uses climate change as a political tool and that they do not really care about the environment. Liberals care about control first and foremost, and everything else comes second, including the well-being of people.

But in the end, you can't fight facts. The total carbon emissions released into the atmosphere by man since the 1800s has been equivalent to just one of earth's historical major volcanic eruptions.[10] After you drop this truth bomb at the cocktail party, if you so choose to lay further destruction to your leftist small-talk-debate-opponent, you can facetiously suggest that the EPA should do more to curb volcanic eruptions by saying something along the lines of "I think it is downright government negligence that has led to these unregulated eruptions. At the very least, we should tax Mother Nature for these emissions, and if need be, even create an oversight committee or government regulation to keep nature in line."

Congratulations, leftists. Well played. I hope you enjoyed your run thus far though, because this is where it ends.

Solution

Shut up Al Gore, you are touching on economic terrorism. We must fight back against the "science" of global warming by doing our own research and proving we are not just sheeple[11] who mindlessly follow what our government tells us without question. We need to illustrate how the earth's current warming (or cooling as the left purported in the 1980s) is mostly natural and not man-made. We must counter the crap science that links global warming to man's activities. One hundred thousand years ago the earth was covered by ice and there were no CFC's or manmade carbon emissions then. And guess what? The ice still melted.

GUN CONTROL

"For target shooting, that's okay. Get a license and go to the range. For defense of the home, that's why we have police departments."

JAMES BRADY, FORMER ASSISTANT TO THE PRESIDENT AND PRESS SECRETARY UNDER RONALD REAGAN

Brady was permanently injured during an assassination attempt on Ronald Reagan (ironically after the shooting, armed men rushed in to secure the scene)

"A well-regulated Militia, being necessary to the security of a free State, the right of the people to keep and bear Arms, shall not be infringed."

SECOND AMENDMENT, UNITED STATES CONSTITUTION

"I don't care if you want to hunt. I don't care if you think it's your right. I say, 'Sorry... We have had enough as a nation. You are not allowed to own a gun, and if you do own a gun I think you should go to prison."

ROSIE O'DONNELL

"I would never invade the United States. There would be a gun behind every blade of grass."

ISOROKU YAMAMOTO, COMMANDER-IN-CHIEF OF THE JAPANESE COMBINED FLEET DURING WORLD WAR II

"When seconds count, the cops are just minutes away."

UNKNOWN

(and one of my favorite quotes after experiencing a break-in personally)

LIBERAL

The Second Amendment does not give citizens the right to keep and bear arms, but rather allows the state to keep a militia, like the National Guard. Individuals do not need guns for protection because it is the role of local and federal government to protect the people through law enforcement and the military. Additional gun control laws are necessary to stop gun violence and limit the number of guns possibly available to criminals. More guns mean more violence, and if you ban guns, or make them more difficult to purchase, less criminals will get their hands on them.

CONSERVATIVE

As Americans, we live under the Constitution, which lists God-given rights and liberties. One of these liberties is guaranteed in the Second Amendment: the right to "keep and bear arms." The Supreme Court has upheld[12] this right. This echoes the sentiment of our founding fathers' belief that citizens have the absolute right to defend themselves; therefore, citizens have the right to keep and bear arms. There are too many gun control laws, and additional laws will not lower crime rates because criminals, by their very definition, disregard the law. More gun laws place additional obstacles on law-abiding citizens. More guns in the hands of law-abiding citizens statistically mean less crime.

In another op-ed I recently wrote on News Rep:

When the Second Amendment was ratified in 1791 the founding fathers made is simple. "A well-regulated Militia, being necessary to the security of a free State, the right of the people to keep and bear Arms, shall not be infringed." Note the sometimes-inconspicuous commas between each subject denoting that; militia, free state, and the right of the people are each individually protected, and the Supreme Court in Heller vs. DC agreed.

The anti-gun movement argues, "There were no AR-15's when the second amendment was written." That is obviously true, but irrelevant. When the Bill of Rights was ratified, there was no internet but that is protected by the First Amendment, also the average citizen possessed the same weaponry as the standing military, including artillery. At the same time, young children also carried those guns to school, resulting in zero school shootings, so to me, that dog don't hunt. The next talking point regurgitated by David Hogg and other liberal pawns is that the AR-15 is a weapon of war, and therefore, should not be available to the general population. Yes, it is, but that is why it is protected. Nearly every firearm at one point has been "military grade" and used for war. I realize this is politically unpopular to say in our current climate of appease-ment, but the point of the Second Amendment is in fact to allow we the people the armament and capability to wage a war against a potential tyrannical government (who will undoubtedly have AR's and more). So, when the left says that because AR-15's are weapons of war and therefore should be banned, your display of profound ignorance demonstrates conclusively you are not informed enough for a legitimate opinion on the matter.

More predictable and polarizing are politicians that weigh in after every shooting with new bills rooted in much of the same misinformation that perpetuates the gun divide in America. In fact, Harvard released a study that gun legislation jumps 15% in the immediate aftermath of mass shootings. The Sandy Hook tragedy is the prime example. Connecticut, my home and ironically, the Constitution state, passed sweeping legislation with heavy restrictions, registration requirements and bans. Certainly, catered to the all blue constituency; the bill, SB1160 passed with even Republican support. Just like you should never grocery shopping when hungry, representatives should never legislate on emotion.

The main problem with this type of knee-jerk governing, in Connecticut's case, nothing in the bill would have affected a single aspect of the Sandy Hook shooting that spawned the legislation, and this is not unique to that instance. The premise behind and the notion that, "If we make it harder to obtain/own guns we will all be safer" sounds appealing, but haven't we tried this with drugs? Heroin and meth are still illegal yet here they are, producing a new pandemic in our country. This type of legislation is what left-leaning politicians think actually improves our society, but it is a complete distraction from addressing the root causes of the problem. Reactionary legislation like this is as futile as making murder more illegal. According to the Crime Prevention Research Center, "gun free zones" have been the target of more than 98% of all mass shootings. The case in Aurora, Colorado displays this, the shooter didn't go to the theater closest to his house or the one with the largest audience, he chose the one that did not allow guns. So, to the enlightened representatives, what law can you pass to make criminals obey laws, they do not like them Sam I am.

If laws actually stopped criminals from committing crime we wouldn't be having this argument. Chicago makes gun owner-

ship virtually impossible yet is deadlier than Iraq was at the height of the war. Followed by Baltimore, New York, Los Angeles, bastions of liberal gun policies have shockingly high crime. Preposterous? Would you be shocked if I told you Australia's gun ban had zero effect on the homicide rate? That zero percent of mass shootings where done by NRA members? In fact, in states that adopted concealed carry, murders dropped by 8.5%, rapes dropped 5%, aggravated assaults dropped 7% and robberies dropped 3%. I'll bet the far left would agree if they actually did real research instead of patting themselves on their backs for useless legislation.

What our "well-meaning liberal friends" (to quote Reagan) never mention is the number of times a day that private gun ownership prevents or deters crime. Why else would the Golden Globes, celebrities and high-ranking members of the government be protected by these men visibly armed with guns? Are their lives more important than our children's who are merely guarded by a sign printed by the lowest municipal bidder that ferociously states "This is a gun free zone"? The same ivory tower elites who scoff at my desire to be able to outfit a small militia at a moment's notice ironically make their millions in large part by glorifying guns. As much as I would love the hand of irony to slap them in the face, I don't fault them. Guns are cool, people like them and its sells movie tickets, capitalism, another conservative policy. They must certainly realize that James Bond being armed with a sternly worded letter from the UN doesn't sell as well as a rocket launcher.

This is a deep fracture in our nation's culture, it won't be solved by legislation and it won't be solved by demagoguery. Gun owners: our guns will never be outright confiscated, and the Second Amendment will never be repealed, unless we give *in to emotion. There are over 300 million guns in America, and the same people who trust the government don't realize that the government can't even control the guns they were supposed to track in Operation Fast and Furious. It is foolish to pretend they can control those on our streets. To set the record straight, the NRA is not pro-gun violence and to say that is absurd. No one is for gun violence. The real enemy is creeping gradualism, gun owners become tolerant or complacent to tiny new legislation that eats away at our ability to own, carry or buy firearms, and the left has made it abundantly clear this will continue. I am writing as a practitioner of my rights via the Second Amendment and want to close with this thought: If you don't like guns, don't buy them, if you do, buy till your heart's content. But when you have over 30 reports of a nut job to local and federal authorities, as we did in Florida, maybe hold the authorities accountable, rather than trying to implicate an entire population of America, who have done nothing wrong. Simple enough right? If both sides would honestly debate this issue on the merits of fact rather than emotion, we would find we are much closer than we think.*

Think about the impact of creeping gradualism and social influence. Hitler made every German register their firearms in the interest of safety. He then confiscated the firearms once he knew who had them.[13] Extreme example? Perhaps, but the Second Amendment is in place to prevent the government from enslaving its citizens—exactly what Hitler accomplished. Hitler first banned guns under the premise that "it was safer for everyone if no one had them." When the Germans and other citizens were unarmed, he killed millions.

We cannot say the founders foresaw Hitler, but they did understand the perils of an unarmed citizenry throughout history. This was made clear when Thomas Jefferson stated, "The strongest reason for the people to retain the right to keep and bear arms is, as a last resort, to protect themselves against tyranny in government."

Benjamin Franklin also opined on the matter when he said, "Democracy is two wolves and a lamb voting on what to have for lunch. Liberty is a well-armed lamb contesting the vote."

Our founding fathers understood that arms in the hands of citizens were the last resort when a government turned to tyranny, yet the left has abandoned the wisdom of our founders and pushes for more gun control.

For liberals, it's not about guns, it's just about control. The left may publicly state that they are trying to pass gun laws for the protection of children, or other emotional causes much like my home state of Connecticut has done along with the inner cities and many more, but their push for gun control is merely an outgrowth in their support for bigger government and more government control—over everything. Liberals must understand that you cannot legislate personal responsibility.

Conventional wisdom can simply point to the liberal meccas that have passed massive gun control measures like Chicago where their annual murder rate is higher than that in the Iraq and Afghanistan wars combined. So many of the recent shootings have occurred in "gun free" zones because criminals, by definition, will not abide by laws. If you are willing to commit murder, will a "gun free" sign stand in your way? On the other side, consider Plano, Texas, the unofficial "gun" capitol of America with more guns per capita than just about another city, with one of the lowest murder rates in the country... but I digress.

Nowhere else in the political landscape is the philosophical divide between right and left more apparent. Liberals want more government control because they believe that government is the answer, but conservatives want more individual freedoms and liberties because they know that the power in this republic rests and should rest with its citizens. That said, all parties must understand that with liberty comes tragedy, but to remove liberty will not eliminate tragedy, it will increase it.

Solution

Limit regulations and gun control to a bare minimum necessary to keep firearms away from those convicted of violent crimes and those not mentally stable enough to carry, and then actually enforce those regulations. Submit to the left's call for background checks and proper identification to purchase a gun, but only if the left will consent to the same for the right to vote (both have equal protection under our Constitution). If you don't like guns, then don't buy them. Owning firearms is a God-given right, not a privilege, but with it comes the burden of responsibility.

HEALTH CARE

"I predict future happiness for Americans if they can prevent the government from wasting the labors of the people under the pretense of taking care of them."

PRESIDENT THOMAS JEFFERSON

"If history is any indication, the actual cost [of Obamacare] will likely be several trillion dollars... [We] believe the health care bill will be the final nail in the coffin of the US economy and will just about guarantee that we will see hyperinflation by the year 2015."

NATIONAL INFLATION ASSOCIATION

"If CBO scored the mandate as taxes, the bill dies, ok? ... lack of transparency is a huge political advantage and basically, you know, call it the stupidity of the American voter or whatever, but basically, that was really, really critical to getting this thing to pass."

JONATHAN GRUBER, ONE OF THE
ARCHITECTS OF OBAMACARE

LIBERAL

The left believes that health care is a right[14] and supports free or low-cost, government-controlled health care at taxpayers' expense. There are millions of Americans who can't afford health care and are, therefore, deprived. The government should provide equal health care benefits for all, regardless of ability to pay and those who can afford to pay should pay for those who cannot.

CONSERVATIVE

Health care is not a right. The right supports a competitive, free market health care system. Conservatives believe that paying for health care and health insurance is a choice one has in a free society. Free, low-cost and single payer government-run programs (socialized medicine) results in higher costs and reduced service and quality of care. Government oversight will stifle innovation; thus, health care should remain privatized.

The government had their shot at running health care, and it is on full display: the US Department of Veterans Affairs is a disaster.

Once again, the battleground is driven by ideological differences. The left believes that government knows best and can provide for its citizens more fairly than the private market. The right believes that we are all inherently free, and with that freedom comes the freedom of choice: the freedom to choose to have health insurance, to choose one's own doctor and to decide on one's care and treatment plan should one become sick.

The intent of the health care bill was never to insure; it was for the government to take control of 1/6 of the economy. There are two factors in this issue: the cost of health insurance and the cost of actual health care. The Affordable Care Act (ACA) did nothing to address the latter. Most of the reason health insurance costs what it does is because of the unregulated costs associated with care; addressing one without the other is futile.

The left's stance is especially ironic in two ways. First, with the Affordable Care Act, liberals say they want all citizens to prove they are insured, but weirdly they don't think it's necessary to require all citizens to prove they are citizens. Second, the left is adamant that health care is a right, which is not included in the Constitution, yet is so opposed to the right to keep and bear arms, which *is* included in the Constitution.

The bottom line is that I would love for everyone to have health insurance, but health care is not a right, no matter how many times the left will try to convince America that it is. It is your right is to shoot for the moon and that may include getting a job that offers health care.

Though the American people were sold a bill that was supposed to make health care more affordable and accessible, since the passing of the Affordable Care Act health care has become less affordable and less accessible. Sure, the left still touts that "20 million more people are insured," but at what cost? The Democrats passed a law mandating people to buy insurance and then bragged about the number of people who complied with the new law. Does that sound ridiculous? Furthermore, while the net number of people insured rose slightly, this does not translate to success of the bill. Many of the people who signed up through the Affordable Care Act were in fact previously insured, liked their plans and their doctors and wanted to keep their plans or doctors, but as a result of the massive overhaul of our health care industry (1/6 of the US economy) they lost coverage and had no other option; many are not pleased with the new care options. Medicaid was then expanded to a near inoperable level to accommodate those who could not afford insurance, hindering that program as well.

First, record number of insurance companies pulled out of the government markets and premiums nearly doubled for most people, causing many of the newly insured to be covered under Medicaid, funded not by the individual but by tax payer subsidies (you and I are paying for it, not the individual). Second, those who have actually purchased health care under Obamacare, due to the lack of options and price, generally elected to have a high deductible to offset a high monthly premium (monthly payment). As a result, their deductibles have sky rocketed to sometimes as high as $10,000. This means that if you want to use medical services during a fiscal year, the first $10,000 of expenses come directly out of your wallet. So, if you spend less than your deductible, (say $9,000) in a given year, your insurance will not have covered a dime. Add that figure to your monthly premium (say $600 dollars) and at the end of that year you will have paid the insurance company $7,200 and the medical community $9,000, none of which will be reimbursed. The out of pocket expense—$16,200—is an unrealistic number. But if the Democratic Party had not mandated you to by insurance, you would only be out of pocket the $9,000 and would never have had to pay a monthly premium. But again, I digress.

SOLUTION

You guessed it: get government out of the way. While Obamacare has dealt a devastating blow to folks with preexisting conditions, we are now on the hook for it. I don't like the idea of the tax payer on the hook for people with pre-existing conditions, but we elected a government that put those policies in place and now must face the music; we broke it and we bought, it to leave them out in the cold would be unethical. We must separate out the pre-existing condition pool and have that, and that, only subsidized while the remainder of the industry is privatized. Allow the free market to prevail and give citizens the right to control their own health care decisions. President Trump's recent repeal of the individual mandate is, for lack of better words, kick ass. Let each person prioritize the importance of health care in his or her life and hold individuals financially accountable for their decisions.

SECURITY SCREENING (IE. TSA, IMMIGRATION AND HOMELAND SECURITY)

"...Arabs, Muslims and South Asians are no more likely than whites to be terrorists."

AMERICAN CIVIL LIBERTIES UNION

"I'm putting the people on notice that are coming here from Syria as part of this mass migration, that if I win, if I win, they're going back."

(THEN CANDIDATE) PRESIDENT DONALD
TRUMP

LIBERAL

It is wrong to profile people, period. Selection of people for extra security screening must be completely random. Using other criteria, such as ethnicity, region or religion is discriminatory and offensive to certain groups (ie. Arabs and Muslims), who are generally innocent and law-abiding. Terrorists don't fit a profile.

CONSERVATIVE

Choosing passengers randomly for extra security searches is not an effective use of resources. Rather, profiling and intelligence analytics based on various factors should be used to single out passengers for extra screening. Those who do not meet the criteria for suspicion should not be subjected to intense screening. The terrorists currently posing a threat to the US are primarily Muslim men between the ages of eighteen and thirty-eight. Our resources should be focused on this group while not ruling out additional groups.

The American left wants us to hire and extend opportunities to people of certain racial or ethnic groups through affirmative action, and if we don't we are labeled as racist. However, stating that we cannot use the same criteria for security screening seems idiotic to me. Do you see any inconsistencies in the left's policies?

When President Bush's Transportation Secretary, Norman Mineta—the only Democrat serving in his cabinet—was asked on "60 Minutes" if a 70-year-old white woman from Vero Beach should receive the same level of scrutiny as a Muslim from Jersey City, he said, "Basically, I would hope so."

How many 70-year-old white women have blown up planes? We are currently spending too many resources screening everyone. We are collecting so much data that we can't effectively analyze it. Too many people slip through the cracks, such as the San Bernardino shooter, the Boston bomber and many more. Would you rather be offended, or would you rather be dead?

SOLUTION

Start profiling based on statistical data. It's time to stop worrying who is offended and start worrying about who is affected.

IMMIGRATION

"Remember, remember always that all of us, and you and I especially are descended from immigrants and revolutionaries."

PRESIDENT FRANKLIN D. ROOSEVELT

"America was indebted to immigration for her settlement and prosperity. That part of America which had encouraged them most had advanced most rapidly in population, agriculture and the arts."

PRESIDENT JAMES MADISON

"Amnesty is a big billboard, a flashing billboard, to the rest of the world that we don't really mean our immigration law."

RICHARD LAMM, FORMER DEMOCRATIC
GOVERNOR OF COLORADO

"Anyone who is in the United States illegally is subject to deportation."

PRESIDENT DONALD TRUMP

LIBERAL

The left supports an increase in immigration (legal or illegal) and amnesty for those who are in the US illegally. Liberals also believe that "undocumented immigrants" have a right to social programs, such as educational and health benefits, financial aid, welfare, Social Security, Medicare and Medicaid and the right to vote. They believe there is no difference in the rights of American citizens and illegal immigrants.

CONSERVATIVE

The right supports legal immigration and opposes amnesty for those who enter the US illegally. Those who break the law by entering the US illegally do not have the same rights as those who obey the law and enter legally. The federal government should secure the borders and enforce current immigration law.

The left is up in arms that President Donald Trump is beginning to build a wall along the southern border and deport illegal immigrants. But the reason why he can do that is because both Bill and Hillary Clinton called for it in the nineties; Senator Hillary Clinton, along with then Senator Barrack Obama and many more, voted to fund and authorize a border wall. And since the president's job is to "faithfully execute the laws as passed by Congress," need I say more?

Immigration is a complex issue encompassing border security, immigration reform and the issue of amnesty. It's important to clarify that illegal aliens are not immigrants, they are criminals. The immigration issue and border security are pressing matters that Washington needs to address immediately. Regardless of President Obama's unilateral amnesty attempt, we are still a nation governed by laws. Now before you get up in arms about this, how would you react to someone breaking into your house, going into your refrigerator, taking your kid's lunch and then sitting on your couch to watch *Shark Week*? Would you invite that person to stay or would you call the police? Illegal immigration is no different.

It seems like common sense that we shouldn't allow people here illegally, but unfortunately the left is clouding our judgment by pushing the narrative that illegal immigration is good for the economy, particularly agriculture, and if you oppose it you have no morality. The additional irony is that for years the left has said that people who come here illegally have no other option because they have no opportunity in their home countries and are fleeing from inhuman conditions to give their families a better life. While this is true, the very second that President Trump allegedly called these countries "shit holes," the left jumped on the band wagon of saying that "these are great and prosperous countries." To which the majority of America responded, "Well, why the hell can't we send illegal immigrants back to them then?"

The left works tirelessly to make immigration an emotional issue, where they tie enforcing our laws to "splitting families" and say things like, "We are the undocumented people's last hope." They make immigration into a humane society commercial where it's just human nature to feel bad for them, which is in fact how most people feel. If only people would realize that the left isn't pushing for amnesty because they care about those people, but because they will gain millions of votes by doing so.

SOLUTION

The government needs to step up and do its job. Seal the borders at any cost and give the option for everyone who came here illegally to become citizens with stipulations that will benefit America. Since it is nearly impossible to seek out and deport all illegal immigrants, first go after the ones who commit additional crimes like President Trump is doing. But do it humanely; create a system that allows illegal immigrants who have otherwise not committed any additional crimes to come out of the shadows and become citizens in a way that benefits America and restrict their right to vote or receive benefits for a period until they have contributed to our economy. People respect things, including rights and privileges, that they have earned.

There is a price that those who broke the law to come here must endure. Those who come here legally would have the same option as always. Prior to this proposal, all illegal immigrants would have a grace period of 30 days to leave the country at will with the option to come in legally after the law is passed. After all that, make legal immigration more accessible and place heavy fines and penalties on businesses that employ illegal immigrants.

RELIGION & GOVERNMENT

LIBERAL

Support the separation of church and state as constitutional law. Religious expression has no place in government or public spaces, especially pertaining to Christianity. The two should be completely separate, and the government should not support religious expression in any way. All reference to God in public and government spaces should be removed.

CONSERVATIVE

The phrase "separation of church and state" is not in the Constitution. The First Amendment to the Constitution states that "Congress shall make no law respecting an establishment of religion, or prohibiting the free exercise thereof..." This prevents the government from establishing a national church and denomination. However, it does not prohibit God, prayer or even the Ten Commandments from being acknowledged in schools and government buildings...or on our currency. Symbols of Christian heritage should not be removed from public and government spaces. The government should not interfere with religion and religious freedom. We are one nation under God.

Our country was founded on Judeo-Christian teachings, so why is there such an issue with it? Because religion tightens the morals of society and the left sees that as oppression. Liberals want society to have loose morals so that people look to the government for guidance, not the Bible.

The left is also happy to classify people who protest Planned Parenthood as religious extremists and terrorists but will not even identify the increasing Muslim threat to America that is characterized by violent extremism.

SOLUTION

Everyone has the freedom to believe in and follow whatever religion they want to as long as it does not directly affect or harm others; being offended is not grounds to ban a particular religion. Like it or not, this is a Christian nation and those are the values that this country was founded on. It is time for us to stop this propaganda that Christianity is evil.

SAME-SEX MARRIAGE AND HOMOSEXUALITY

"If the Supreme Court says that you have the right to consensual [gay] sex within your home, then you have the right to bigamy, you have the right to polygamy, you have the right to incest, you have the right to adultery. You have the right to anything. Does that undermine the fabric of our society? I would argue yes, it does. ... That's not to pick on homosexuality. It's not, you know, man on child, man on dog, or whatever the case may be. It is one thing."

RICK SANTORUM (PRESIDENTIAL
CANDIDATE)

"From a religious point of view, if God had thought homosexuality is a sin, he would not have created gay people."

GOVERNOR HOWARD DEAN

LIBERAL

Homosexuality is natural. Some people are simply born gay. We should embrace it and even encourage people to try it. Marriage is the union of people who love each other and is not restricted to one-man-one-woman relationships. It should be extended to gay, lesbian, bisexual and transgender couples. Laws to the contrary of this belief deny citizens of equal rights.

CONSERVATIVE

Marriage is between a man and a woman. Specifically, a relationship comprised of one man and one woman. To extend the right of marriage beyond this strict Judeo-Christian definition would lead to a slippery slope that would eventually deteriorate and perhaps destroy the traditional values of western society.

While many may disagree on views about homosexuality, many moderate conservatives believe individuals are born with their sexual orientation. I personally struggle with homosexuality because of an incident I experienced as a young child; but nevertheless, I do not advocate for laws against it. I agree with civil unions for gays and leave the church to decide on the sanctity of marriage. What you do in your bedroom is your business, but how others feel about is also *their* right, and that doesn't make people bigots, it is just an opinion. Gay marriage will not make the stock market crash, government is best when it governs least, and we need to apply this logic to this topic.

SOLUTION

Allow civil unions between same-sex couples but keep religious marriage between one man and one woman or as the church deems appropriate. Conservatives will be afforded the opportunity to keep marriage defined in Judeo-Christian terms, and liberals will be afforded the ability to allow homosexuals to enter civil unions that will have equal legal standing to marriage.

THE GLOBAL WAR ON TERRORISM & NATIONAL SECURITY

"As a result of the [9/11] attack and the killing of nearly 3,000 innocent people, we invaded two countries and killed innocent people in their countries...Radical Christianity is just as threatening as radical Islam in a country like America."

ROSIE O'DONNELL

"On September 11, 2001, America felt its vulnerability even to threats that gather on the other side of the Earth. We resolved then, and we are resolved today, to confront every threat from any source that could bring sudden terror and suffering to America."

PRESIDENT GEORGE W. BUSH

LIBERAL

Global warming is a bigger threat than terrorism to America. Terrorism is the result of the United States' foreign policy that often-times backed dictators and despots in order to progress our agenda. More recently, our post-Cold War foreign policy of basing troops in the Middle East and taking a more active role in Arab countries has caused backlash among some Muslims. Apologies, negotiations, foreign aid and a dramatic shift in our foreign policy are the best tools to deal with terrorism. Iraq and Afghanistan were peaceful places before America invaded. The American military action will only make those countries worse, and if America were to cease military action in those areas they will also leave us alone. Terrorists should be given civil rights and tried in civilian courts.

CONSERVATIVE

Terrorism is the greatest threat to the United States. Islamic extremists will never surrender in their crusade to destroy Israel and the West. Terrorists must be sought out, killed or captured and put in the detention facility on Naval Station Guantanamo Bay. The use of intelligence collection and military force are the best ways to defeat terrorism around the world; while nation building would be ideal, it has not been effective. Captured terrorists should be treated as enemy combatants and tried in military courts. The use of negotiation and peace talks are necessary to divert or end a conflict, but force should never be ruled out and should always be on clear display. Although foreign aid can be an effective tool of the State Department, we should require more contingencies for receiving states such as the compensation of national resources.

As an Iraq War veteran, I understand that the war on terrorism, specifically Operations Iraqi Freedom and Enduring Freedom, is complex, multi-faceted and oftentimes nuanced. The West must understand that Islam is as much a political ideology of conquest as it is a religion. Since 700 AD and the coming of the prophet Muhammad, the mission and the teachings of the Quran have been to usher in a world without infidels and to spread their ideology. While many Muslims do not wish to harm or even influence others, many more are happy to do this peacefully through simply relocating and procreating faster than the local populous; some will even carry it out militantly. As we have seen with the increased sexual assaults across Europe recently by refugees, women are viewed as property and tools for breeding in Islam, which does not correspond with western values.

I also want to express that America's military must and will prevail over Islamic extremism. While many of the terrorists I encountered in Iraq were part of a bigger ideology, unable to extend threats beyond Iraq, others were skilled, proficient and highly organized combatants with the means necessary to attack the United States at home and our allies abroad. We are seeing this today with ISIS and their affiliates attacking countries all over the world. These individual terrorists must be sought out and destroyed, with more concern for success and less for collateral damage.

Yet some on the left, and even a group of top military officials, believe we can simply talk our way to victory by making the terrorists like us. As Admiral William H. McRaven said about the global war on terror, "The US cannot kill its way to victory."

Actually Admiral, you can kill your way to victory. If you destroy your enemy then there is no more enemy, and you have won; that is the basic rule of war. Ironically that is our enemies' motto, and we should be prepared to do the same. It is highly prejudicial that members of our government would honestly believe that we can negotiate with people whose only goal in life is to kill Americans. It's time to be realistic and realize that the only way to deal with terrorists is to kill them before they kill us.

I have confronted these terrorists face-to-face on the battlefield and believe that some of the terrorists will stop at nothing in their goal to destroy western civilization. Wake up, liberals! We have the world's strongest, most powerful military and it's time we use it...on our terms.

Too many times when asked what it would take to change their minds about military action in the Middle East, liberals say something like, "Well, I think if there was a major tragedy I might change my mind." Aside from 9/11, the American service member has endured tragedy every day for the last decade and a half for your safety so that you wouldn't have to, does that count? While many in my generation are happy to let others serve on their behalf, those who have not faced this threat should not discount it for lack of their personal experience. I fear that my generation would not be able to answer a call like the previous generations did for World War I and World War II, or even Vietnam.

Solution

Theodore Roosevelt said, "Walk softly and carry a big stick." Sometimes we must use that stick and that time is now. If you don't want to kill bad guys, then don't join the military. But when our soldiers come home from war after putting their life on the line for our country's safety, you need to start treating them with respect and stop complaining about a war that is being fought by a volunteer military. You also must understand that sometimes when we come back from war, we may have feelings that do not align with a perfect world view. It's not always post-traumatic stress, sometimes it's just a view that is hardened by war.

WELFARE & ENTITLEMENT PROGRAMS

"If the people cannot trust their government to do the job for which it exists—to protect them and to promote their common welfare—all else is lost."

PRESIDENT BARACK OBAMA

"I don't want to make black people's lives better by giving them somebody else's money; I want to give them the opportunity to go out and earn the money."

RICK SANTORUM, CAMPAIGN STOP IN
IOWA, JANUARY 2, 2012

LIBERAL

Welfare and entitlement programs are necessary to help those in need and are good for the economy. Welfare is a safety net that provides for the needs of the poor and for people who may be down on their luck. It is necessary to bring fairness and compassion to the American economy.

CONSERVATIVE

Democrats buy votes by promising these benefits at the taxpayer expense. Welfare and entitlement programs should only be for those with serious disabilities and handicaps, short-term periods of unemployment and senior citizens that are actually "senior." Although recipients of government aid generally spend their money on goods and services, thus placing money into the economy, there is no net gain because that money was initially taken from the economy in the form of taxes in the first place. While it is understood that sometimes people need a safety net, reasonable and limited subsidies should be part of our nation's benevolence, but reforms should be undertaken to prevent government dependency.

Prior to the Civil War, people designated by skin color were provided housing and food in exchange for labor. Now more than 160 years later another group of people, this time designated by economic class, have been given housing and food by the candidate that promises more housing and food, essentially buying votes. When Republicans ended slavery based on race, did Democrats bring it underground and rebrand it using entitlement benefits?

My thoughts on this are very simple: if we do not reform the system now, it will crash later. My plea to people is that they vote responsibly now to ensure longevity of the essential system lest we are left with nothing later on. Let's be frank: both our debt and spending are wildly out of control. While some point fingers at regulation, spending, foreign aid and Congressional pay raises, the real problem is our entitlement programs. Entitlements accounted for more than 60 percent of the national budget in 2014.[15] That is the largest percentage of national debt, followed only by the money we pay on interest to the nation's debt. Compounding matters, the nation's debt is fueled by our entitlement programs. When looking at the figures, we must be honest with ourselves and get people off America's dole. We cannot afford these programs and my generation cannot sustain these government handouts. As our population ages, my generation will be carrying the burden as we will be strapped with the high taxes and deep cuts necessary to support these programs. This is the number one fiscal issue our representatives must tackle, because in the end we are the ones who are going to suffering the most for it. But how do you take it away? What will people do? How will they live?

Solution

Our representatives need to drastically reform entitlements. In 1935 when social security was started, the average life expectancy was sixty-one years[16] and now it is almost eighty. We must raise the required age for social security and reform Medicare spending. This is a burden that cannot be ignored. As an American you pay into social security your whole life and it must be there when you are eligible; at this rate it will not be there for my generation. I am fine with not receiving that benefit until I am seventy, rather than not receiving it at all.

For other entitlement programs, they should be available only for those who truly cannot take care of themselves, such as the mentally ill and children. Those who seek unemployment or general welfare should have access to a safety net, but perhaps those programs should include incentives to eventually move to self-sufficiency. Job programs, municipal work and perhaps a monthly reduction in benefits over a set period of time would serve to avoid complacency. We must redefine society's definitions of "needs" and "wants" before everyone starts to become dependent on the government.

MULTICULTURALISM AND RACE RELATIONS

"Fortunately, the time has long passed when people liked to regard the United States as some kind of melting pot, taking men and women from every part of the world and converting them into standardized, homogenized Americans. We are, I think, much more mature and wise today. Just as we welcome a world of diversity, so we glory in an America of diversity -- an America all the richer for the many different and distinctive strands of which it is woven."

VICE PRESIDENT HUBERT HUMPHREY

"There can be no fifty-fifty Americanism in this country. There is room here for only 100% Americanism, only for those who are Americans and nothing else."

PRESIDENT THEODORE ROOSEVELT

"There is not a liberal America and a conservative America - there is the United States of America. There is not a black America and a white America and Latino America and Asian America - there's the United States of America."

PRESIDENT BARACK OBAMA

LIBERAL

We live in a salad bowl, not a melting pot. Immigrants and other ethnic groups should retain their individual culture and traditions, and mainstream American culture should give way to these differences and encourage them. It is racist, prejudice or non-inclusive to speak ill of any culture despite conflictions with personal beliefs. Minorities need help obtaining employment, receiving promotions and gaining admission to higher education because the proverbial playing field is stacked against them.

Conservative

We live in a melting pot, not a salad bowl. Immigrants and other ethnic groups are free to believe what they want but should adopt American values, culture and traditions. We encourage everyone to honor their own cultures and customs but understand that they come second to American values. Minorities are equal. We are all individuals and should be treated as such, and to do otherwise is racist. Equal opportunity does not mean equal achievement.

Race drove the 2008 and 2012 elections of Barack Obama. The right did not make an issue of Barack Obama's race, the left did under the guise that not voting for him was racist. How many times did you hear someone say, "Well, I just think it would be cool to see the first African-American president elected." Sound familiar? Of course it does! I have even had conservative friends that openly stated they feared Barack Obama would not get a second term and that the rest of the world would assume that was because we are a racist society, never mind his actual governing record! Out of these concerns, many voted for the not-even-one-term-senator and already failed president *because* he was black. But no, that's not racism is it?

Wake up, America. Voting for someone simply because he or she is black, white or green is just as racist as *not* voting for that person for the same reason. I didn't like President Obama because his policies were historical failures, it had nothing to do with him being half black. My generation must put an end to the practice of rewarding individuals for their skin color. Logically, that is the same as *punishing* individuals for their skin color. Note how I say "individual." That's because America is a nation of citizens, not of ethnic groups. We are not divided into subcategories of Americans; we are all one group of Americans and should hold a common goal—the betterment of America. This rally cry is what got President Trump elected: "America First."

I have been to more than fifty countries, and many of them are governed by groups and religions, not governments. I saw firsthand the perils of an ethnic group-based society. Trust me, you don't want to live in that kind of divisive society. We must end the hyphenated American syndrome (As Theodore Roosevelt said, the "fifty-fifty" American). Groupism and multiculturalism are tearing our society apart. If you live here you should be American, and that is something to be proud of, not scoffed at. Isn't that why people come here in the first place, for the American dream?

SOLUTION

Our generation must insist that individuals be treated as individuals and rewarded and promoted on talent and merit. Affirmative action and the trend to live in a hyphenated, fifty-fifty American society must end. The best man or woman gets the job.

These are the major issues of the American political battlegrounds. Despite what you have been sold in the media, from your professors or colleges, this is the reality of each side. There are issues on both sides that have masked their true meaning, but those are the reality of each party. Without a doubt, no matter what party you identify with, there are things on both sides that you both agreed and disagreed with—this is the product of the emerging class of a new generational political faction. Where do you stand?

PART TWO

PERSONAL RESPONSIBILITY

ACCOUNTABILITY, PATRIOTISM & SACRIFICE AND MULTICULTURALISM

CHAPTER ONE
ACCOUNTABILITY AND FAKE NEWS

HOW AND WHY OUR COUNTRY MUST RESTORE ACCOUNTABILITY AT ALL LEVELS

"Democracy requires accountability, and accountability requires transparency."

PRESIDENT BARRACK OBAMA

"I am willing to wager that NRA members are more law abiding than Democrats."

CARL HIGBIE

BEFORE WE CAN EVEN START on the battleground issues, we need to embrace personal accountability that the left has largely pushed out of its agenda. Accountability is what holds a democracy and, thus, our society together—this cannot be over-emphasized. It holds individuals to a personal, professional and moral standard. Without accountability, we could not have a functioning society. This is what the left wants; they are not saying it because it sounds ridiculous, but if they can erode the fiber that holds society together, then they can fill that void by giving citizens the safety net of government, making them more dependent on the very system that is letting them down, thus giving government more control.

You don't believe me? Look at CNN leading the charge in shining armor, on horseback and bearing flags into the battle against Donald Trump's presidency. They ran piece after piece against Brett Kavanaugh despite ALL evidence in his favor. CNN used to be a well-respected, cutting-edge media giant, but it has turned into a propaganda arm with multiple debunked and completely false stories. The prime-time anchors' ratings fall short of *SpongeBob SquarePants* re-runs, and they are even ridiculed by their liberal counterparts. Why? Because they are not accountable to the truth but rather an agenda.

Sadly, as the left becomes more entrenched globally with heavy backers like George Soros, accountability in western civilization and the United States has been waning, thus we are slowly slipping into an inefficient and failing society. Actually remove emotion regardless of your political bearings and think about this rationally. Who is funding, organizing or supporting the groups who advocate things like "pigs in a blanket, fry them like bacon" regarding police officers, who protest Ben Shapiro and other conservatives giving speeches on college campuses, who occupy Wall Street and who support Antifa? It's Democrats and the left!

Samuel Huntington explained in *The Clash of Civilizations* that the West's decline is rooted partly in moral decline. Manifestations include "anti-social behavior, such as crime, drug use, and violence... family decay, including increased rates of divorce, illegitimacy, teenage pregnancy, and single-parent families...general weakening of 'work ethic' and rise of a cult of personal indulgence."[1]

Individuals no longer hold themselves nor others accountable to standards and commitments. As most evident with President Obama's executive action on immigration that President Trump unwound, our government has ignored the Constitution, and representatives have defied their own laws. There was no outrage at this by the mainstream media, but when President Trump began deporting people—at a lower rate than President Obama—and even when he dismantled the Deferred Action for Childhood Arrivals (DACA) policy, the media was up in arms for President Trump actually upholding the law. Who holds the media accountable? President Trump does. The then media say they are "just holding him accountable," and around in circles they go.

I can attest to the fake news of CNN and their ilk. CNN published a story on me that I had said some things on a radio show five years earlier. In full disclosure and ownership, I did say some of the things in context as reported; I have long since apologized for that, and I recognize how wrong it was to make some blanket statements as I did. Many of the issues on those radio interviews I struggled with coming home from war, but I take accountability for that and did so on a very big stage. However, many other things in the headlines may have seemed to be all the worst things, but when put in context, are far more reasonable than portrayed; nevertheless, I owned it and moved on.

What was crazy was that almost all of the reporters I spoke to during this week of chaos were shocked that I just apologized—no excuses, no typical politician "I misspoke" or "I apologize for how this was interpreted." I just said, "Yes, I'm sorry. I was wrong, period." Far more than my own situation, what worried me was that out of the thousands of public figures these reporters had interviewed in their careers, the fact that they were shocked by ownership is an astonishing lapse of accountability in our culture.

The United States has devolved into a nation of excuses as those who make the laws sometimes believe they are above them. The principal "of, by, and for the people" delineates us from third-world nations like Iraq, Nigeria, Venezuela and other similar countries. We cannot start to restore our country without restoring accountability—of ourselves, our society, and our government.

PERSONAL ACCOUNTABILITY

"When we are really honest with ourselves we must admit our lives are all that really belong to us. So it is how we use our lives that determines the kind of men we are."

CÉSAR CHAVEZ

Like so many things in life, the problem and solution start within us. As a member of Generation Y, I witnessed the propaganda blast and how my peers were—and some still are—coddled from pre-school to adulthood. Sadly, we are the generation in which every kid received a trophy. Actual achievement was secondary to recognition. We are the generation that blamed poor grades on teachers; the lack of studying was merely coincidental. Some schools today even propose that we remove grades from the education system, one of the litmus tests of accountability.

Worst of all, we are the generation that expects job offers to come pouring in after we graduate college. The fact that we hold a degree in sociology or gender studies and fail to send out a single résumé is ignored. And some of our parents in large part say, "well it's just a really tough job market." There is a lack of drive and initiative because our rewards were rarely tied to our own achievement.

Growing up we were bombarded with positive reinforcement. The Baby Boomers tied reward to achievement *and* failure, where equal credit was given for effort as success. Imagine getting an "A" on a test solely for sitting in the classroom.

I'm sure everyone had one or two teachers that you hated in school that didn't let you get away with anything. For me, it was my Spanish teacher, "The Gavin", and my wrestling coach, Brad. I hated Gavin when I was his student but looking back I wish there were more teachers like him. Brad was my wrestling coach that never let me cut a corner. To this day I hear, "Carl never half ass anything, whole ass everything." They singlehandedly had the most influence over any other figures in my professional life because they held me accountable, and today I am thankful for that. But that is being discouraged today, and it is hurting our society.

SOCIETAL ACCOUNTABILITY

Once we hold ourselves accountable, we must start holding others in society accountable. This is not an easy task as we have seen President Trump's battle with fake news. We need to not be afraid or intimidated to call someone out, and not be offended when called out ourselves.

In Connecticut there is a very successful investment management company called Bridgewater Associates, and their bedrock principal is accountability. It is widely known across the finance industry as an abrasive and shark-infested environment where members hold each other accountable for even the smallest infractions; being offended is not tolerated and sulking isn't an option because you will be terminated if you don't fix the deficiency immediately. Not even the founder, Ray Dalio, is above taking responsibility for his actions.

Could this type of accountable environment be the root of the company's success?

Many people are offended and appalled by my willingness to publicly call someone out on their bullshit or parade the obvious solution that others want to communicate but don't out of fear of ridicule. What is more disconcerting is that some people will spend more time crying about the offensive nature of the criticism rather than critiquing the issue or even implementing the obvious solution presented in the criticism. Even more ridiculous is that people often agree with many of my frank statements behind closed doors, and once their ego heals the situation is usually solved on the merits of the proposal. Imagine if society, the workforce or even government stopped taking offense by a difference of opinion and simply operated with the efficiency of a group like Bridgewater Associates, where the ego is not tolerated. That would be a fantastic place to start.

In a real-world example, I applied for my pistol permit after moving back to Connecticut in 2014. Initially, despite holding a valid pistol permit in another state and being a former Navy SEAL, I was told that I needed additional credentials to prove I was competent in handling a firearm.[2] After talking to the chief of police, who was very rational about the situation, I was finally able to get the additional and redundant safety course waived and allowed to submit the current qualifications that I possessed in lieu of the previous requirements. Keep in mind that the other state I held my permit in had the same NRA safety course requirements as Connecticut.

I then had to fill out additional paperwork, get finger printed for both state and local agencies, and pay more than $200 in fees.[3] Upon submitting the paperwork I was instructed that I would receive my permit in sixteen to twenty-four weeks. When I informed the bureaucrat behind the counter that according to C.G.S. Section 29-32, the issuing authority has eight weeks to review applications and provide an approval or denial, she became immediately disgruntled and said,

"I'll tell you what the law is, there is a backlog and we are processing permits as fast as we can, sir."

You see, if I were to not register my car on time because of a backlog at work, I would be ticketed or even jailed. So why would a public servant, whose job it is to serve the public, be allowed to keep her job after an incident like this? What's more, when this was brought to the attention of the second selectman, also known as assistant mayor of the town, she was still not fired. I did, however, receive my permit in less than two weeks, so I consider it a win.

While I got what he wanted, how was I able to get my permit back so quickly? Was it because I knew the law and actually spoke up about it? Are these public servants not here to serve the people and assist us in navigating laws, privileges and rights to the best of their ability? The fact that this matter was closed so quickly lends thought to the notion that this is a matter not of a backlog or a lack of resources, but of government not working efficiently and at their own comfortable pace. What would happen to an employee of a financial institution if they blatantly blew off a filing deadline or regulation because they were backlogged? They would be fired and, most likely, their license to work in the industry would be revoked. Why does it seem that civil servants are becoming less civil and acting less like servants? Could it be the lack of accountability tied to our institutions that in large part we have elected or allowed to stay in power?

Laws and social norms are a reflection of what a society decides its members should be accountable to. Social norms or morals are a set of unwritten rules and expectations. Laws are government-imposed parameters on accountability, a mandated code society places upon its members. Since the 1960s, we have cared less and less about holding others accountable to laws and societal norms. Accountability has been shifted from the individual to society as a whole.

Take the example of Trayvon Martin. According to public records of the incident, on February 26, 2012 George Zimmerman noticed

Trayvon Martin walking in between homes in Zimmerman's gated community. Zimmerman grew suspicious as he had never seen Martin in his neighborhood before, and the 17-year-old Martin was looking at homes in the neighborhood and walking incredibly slow for the rainy weather. When Zimmerman confronted Martin, Martin attacked Zimmerman. Zimmerman shot Martin in self-defense, inflicting a fatal wound. After the incident, EMTs treated Zimmerman for wounds he suffered in the fray, and police interrogated him for five hours before releasing him as the facts corroborated his self-defense story.

In the days following the incident, the media and leftists did not blame Martin for attacking Zimmerman. Rather, the media attacked Zimmerman for initiating what the left said as a racially motivated attack. As the media saw it, Martin was a victim of society. NBC went so far as to edit the 9-1-1 call Zimmerman placed in a way to make it seem like he was racist. In reality, Zimmerman did say Martin was black, but he did so in response to the 9-1-1 dispatcher asking him about Martin's race, which NBC edited out.

Zimmerman pursued a defamation suit against NBC for portraying him as a racist by editing the tapes, but the damage was done, convicted in the court of public opinion. All the while no attention was paid to the fact that Martin was on school suspension during the time of the shooting. What was he suspended for? For spraying "WTF" graffiti. When the police searched him after this incident, they reported that they found women's jewelry on Martin, a screwdriver, presumably used as a robbery tool, a marijuana pipe and a plastic bag with marijuana residue in it. These facts went largely unreported. After all, the whole matter is society's fault, according to the media and the left.[4] At least that is the agenda the left wants people to believe.

A more recent example is the shooting of Michael Brown by Officer Darren Wilson in Ferguson, Missouri. Afterward there was rioting and looting on the basis of black people not getting justice, in effect implementing mob rule. It has become very apparent that the officer acted within the confines of the law when Michael Brown reached for the officer's gun, justifying the officer's actions, yet large factions of the black community continued to riot in the streets for the officer's arrest, screaming "hands up don't shoot" and, for some unknown reason to most, to destroy local business establishments. Reverend Al Sharpton wasted no time in inciting this as a race battle rather than a social or even personal issue of conduct. Sharpton could have called on the black community to be more accountable to the youth and not let some of their children grow up to rob a convenient store, assault the business owner and a police officer leading to an altercation that resulted in being shot dead in the street, but that approach would not have fit his race-baiting agenda. Furthermore, this incident was the birth of the Black Lives Matter movement that held a criminal known as Assata Shakur as their prophet—a convicted murderer named, as of 2013, on the FBI's most wanted terror list. During the 2016 campaign for president, both Hillary Clinton and Bernie Sanders legitimized this group by meeting with them, seeking an alliance not because they cared about the issue or cause but because they wanted votes.

This is the impact on a populous that can be fed a narrative to the point where it is accepted over reality. Most people affected by this would argue that they are not prone to propaganda, but they are. These people connect with the cause because the people behind the propaganda feed the emotional narrative to justify the ignorance of facts and reality. This is a dangerous line because once emotions rule our society and not laws, there is no end to the damage that will be done.

When will we stop these foolish games? When we will stop lying to ourselves? When will we stop placing blame on society and instead of on the wrongdoer? It is time we start pointing the finger at individual transgressors. That applies to crimes and the breaking of societal norms. If your co-worker screws up a presentation because he was hungover, then call him on it. If your brother fathers a child out of wedlock, tell him to take responsibility for the child and be a father. If your friend complains about not having enough money, but then debates taking out yet another credit card, stop him and give him an application for a second job. It is time we start holding ourselves and each other to a higher standard.[5]

For the record, I'm not encouraging a lack of compassion or understanding toward others. This is not about being coldhearted, it is simply tough love. Despite what the left says, the right does have compassion for people, and that compassion is what drives us to believe that people can succeed on their own without the help of the government. It starts with personal responsibility.

We hear people making excuses for others every single day and shifting blame to society and circumstances. There are endless examples: "Johnny didn't just misbehave, no, no—it's because the school system refuses to cater to his unique needs," "Aunt Debbie isn't sixty pounds over-weight because she is irresponsible, eats crap, can't add up the calories she is stuffing in her mouth or because she neglects to exercise. No, no—it's because evil fast food chains are opening a drive-through on every corner," "Sam didn't rob that store because he's an unsupervised delinquent. No, no—it's because society didn't provide him with enough opportunities for employment," "Bobby didn't get the job because he doesn't speak proper English, dresses like a gang banger with purple hair. No, no—it's because the business world wants to keep him down." Enough! Society is falling apart because of this nonsense. An entire generation has been ruined by this crap.

"We must reject the idea that every time a law's broken society is guilty rather than the lawbreaker. It is time to restore the American precept that each individual is accountable for his actions."

PRESIDENT RONALD REAGAN

This is an American precept, that individuals control their own destinies, are responsible for their own actions and are beholden only to themselves. As Americans, we are the descendants of the pioneers, the cowboys who conquered the wild west and the fearless immigrants, all of whom found pride in rugged individualism. Where has this spirit gone? Where has our resolve gone today?

It is time we as a society restore it. Generation Y, this is our mandate. We need a backbone. We must reward individualism and personal accountability, and reject collectivism, the spineless notion of allowing our institutions to walk all over us and the left's knee-jerk reaction to blame society. Only when we hold ourselves and others accountable can we embark on the real, much needed change of holding our government accountable.

GOVERNMENT ACCOUNTABILITY

Two and a half centuries ago we fought the Revolutionary War over a 2 percent tax hike on tea. Let that sink in. We fought a war over a 2 two percent tax hike on a beverage. If only our founding fathers could see the blunders of our current government.

We the people do not hold the government accountable largely because we fail to hold ourselves and others in society accountable. This failure is a blunder on a gigantic scale. Without accountability, the government has no limits, enjoys free rein, reckless spending, creates mile-high deficits and attempts to skirt the Constitution. And they tell us it's OK.

Over all the government is a vacuum of accountability and nothing displays that more than the hypocrisy of a political witch-hunt on Donald Trump and on his appointees while ignoring all the collusion, misleading statements and payoffs of the previous administration. An anonymous posting on Reddit summed up the corruption so well that I have quoted it directly. In full disclosure: I was not able to personally confirm every statement, but I was able to confirm the accuracy of the overwhelming majority:

I am passing this on from someone who's connecting some dots with input from sources he cannot reveal.

Here's what it looks like when all the pieces are sewn together.

It smells like conspiracy and treason. Everyone needs to read this. Slowly, and patiently, because it's very important......

From 2001 to 2005 there was an ongoing investigation into the Clinton Foundation.

A Grand Jury had been impaneled.

Governments from around the world had donated to the "Charity".

Yet, from 2001 to 2003 none of those "Donations" to the Clinton Foundation were declared. Now you would think that an honest investigator would be able to figure this out.

Look who took over this investigation in 2005: None other

than James Comey; Coincidence? Guess who was transferred into the Internal Revenue Service to run the Tax Exemption Branch of the IRS? None other than, Lois "Be on The Look Out" (BOLO) Lerner. Isn't that interesting?

But this is all just a series of strange coincidences, right?

Guess who ran the Tax Division inside the Department of Injustice from 2001 to 2005?

No other than the Assistant Attorney General of the United States,
Rod Rosenstein.

Guess who was the Director of the Federal Bureau of Investigation during this time frame?

Another coincidence (just an anomaly in statistics and chances), but it was Robert Mueller.

What do all four casting characters have in common?

They all were briefed and/or were front-line investigators into the Clinton Foundation Investigation.

Another coincidence, right?

Fast forward to 2009....

James Comey leaves the Justice Department to go and cash-in at Lockheed Martin.

Hillary Clinton is running the State Department, official government business, on her own personal email server.

The Uranium One "issue" comes to the attention of the Hillary.

Like all good public servants do, supposedly looking out for America's best interest, she decides to support the decision and approve the sale of 20% of US Uranium to no other than, the Russians.

Now you would think that this is a fairly straight up deal, except it wasn't, America got absolutely nothing out of it.

However, prior to the sales approval, no other than Bill Clinton goes to Moscow, gets paid 500K for a one hour speech; then meets with Vladimir Putin at his home for a few hours.

Ok, no big deal right? Well, not so fast, the FBI had a mole inside the money laundering and bribery scheme.

Robert Mueller was the FBI Director during this time frame? Yep, He even delivered a Uranium Sample to Moscow in 2009.

Who was handling that case within the Justice Department out of the US Attorney's Office in Maryland?

None other than, Rod Rosenstein. And what happened to the informant?
The Department of Justice placed a GAG order on him and threatened to lock him up if he spoke out about it.

How does 20% of the most strategic asset of the United States of America end up in Russian hands when the FBI has an informant, a mole providing inside information to the FBI on the criminal enterprise?

Very soon after; the sale was approved!~145 million dollars in "donations" made their way into the Clinton Foundation from entities directly connected to the Uranium One deal.

Guess who was still at the Internal Revenue Service working the Charitable Division? None other than, - Lois Lerner.

Ok, that's all just another series of coincidences, nothing to see here, right?

Let's fast forward to 2015.

Due to a series of tragic events in Benghazi and after the 9 "investigations" the House, Senate and at State Department, Trey Gowdy who was running the 10th investigation as Chairman of the Select Committee on Benghazi discovers that the Hillary ran the State Department on an unclassified, unauthorized, outlaw personal email server. He also discovered that none of those emails had been turned over when she departed her "Public Service" as Secretary of State which was required by law. He also discovered that there was Top Secret information contained within her personally archived email.

Sparing you the State Departments cover up, the nostrums they floated, the delay tactics that were employed and the outright lies that were spewed forth from the necks of the Kerry State Department, we shall leave it with this...... they did everything humanly possible to cover for Hillary. .

Now this is amazing, guess who became FBI Director in 2013? None other than James Comey; who secured 17 no bid contracts for his employer (Lockheed Martin) with the State Department and was rewarded with a six million dollar thank you present when he departed his employer? Amazing how all those no-bids just went right through at State, huh?

Now he is the FBI Director in charge of the "Clinton Email Investigation" after of course his FBI Investigates the Lois Lerner "Matter" at the Internal Revenue Service and he exonerates her. Nope.... couldn't find any crimes there.

In April 2016, James Comey drafts an exoneration letter of Hillary Rodham Clinton, meanwhile the DOJ is handing out immunity deals like candy. They didn't even convene a Grand Jury!

Like a lightning bolt of statistical impossibility, like a miracle from God himself, like the true "Gangsta" Comey is, James steps out into the cameras of an awaiting press conference on July the 8th of 2016, and exonerates the Hillary from any wrongdoing.

Do you see the pattern?

It goes on and on, Rosenstein becomes Asst. Attorney General, Comey gets fired based upon a letter by Rosenstein, Comey leaks government information to the press, Mueller is assigned to the Russian Investigation sham by Rosenstein to provide cover for decades of malfeasance within the FBI and DOJ and the story continues.

FISA Abuse, political espionage..... pick a crime, any crime, chances are...... this group and a few others did it:

All the same players.

All compromised and conflicted.

All working fervently to NOT go to jail themselves

All connected in one way or another to the Clinton's.

They are like battery acid; they corrode and corrupt everything they touch. How many lives have these two destroyed?

As of this writing, the Clinton Foundation, in its 20+ years of operation of being the largest International Charity Fraud in the history of mankind, has never been audited by the Internal Revenue Service.

Let us not forget that Comey's brother works for DLA Piper, the law firm that does the Clinton Foundation's taxes.

The person that is the common denominator to all the crimes above and still doing her evil escape legal maneuvers at the top of the 3 Letter USA Agencies?

Yep, that would be Hillary R. Clinton.

Now who is LISA BARSOOMIAN? Let's learn a little about Mrs. Lisa H. Barsoomian's background.

Lisa H. Barsoomian, an Attorney that graduated from Georgetown Law, is a protégé of James Comey and Robert Mueller.

Barsoomian, with her boss R. Craig Lawrence, represented Bill Clinton in 1998.

Lawrence also represented:

Robert Mueller three times;
James Comey five times;

Barack Obama 45 times;
Kathleen Sebelius 56 times;
Bill Clinton 40 times; and
Hillary Clinton 17 times.

Between 1998 and 2017, Barsoomian herself represented the FBI at least five times.

You may be saying to yourself, OK, who cares? Who cares about the work history of this Barsoomian woman?

Apparently, someone does, because someone out there cares so much that they've "purged" all Barsoomian court documents for her Clinton representation in Hamburg vs. Clinton in 1998 and its appeal in 1999 from the DC District and Appeals Court dockets (?). Someone out there cares so much that even the internet has been "purged" of all information pertaining to Barsoomian.

Historically, this indicates that the individual is a protected CIA operative. Additionally, Lisa Barsoomian has specialized in opposing Freedom of Information Act requests on behalf of the intelligence community. Although Barsoomian has been involved in hundreds of cases representing the DC Office of the US Attorney, her email address is Lisa Barsoomian at NIH.gov. The NIH stands for National Institutes of Health. This is a tactic routinely used by the CIA to protect an operative by using another government organization to shield their activities.

It's a cover, so big deal right? What does one more attorney with ties to the US intelligence community really matter?

It deals with Trump and his recent tariffs on Chinese steel and aluminum imports, the border wall, DACA, everything coming out of California, the Uni-party unrelenting opposition to President Trump, the Clapper leaks, the Comey leaks, Attorney General Jeff Sessions recusal and subsequent 14 month nap with occasional forays into the marijuana legalization mix .... and last but not least Mueller's never-ending investigation into collusion between the Trump team and the Russians.

Why does Barsoomian, CIA operative, merit any mention?

BECAUSE....

She is Assistant Attorney General Rod Rosenstein's WIFE!

The corruption is unbelievable and in the recusal of Jeff Sessions look at who is running the hen house!!

THE OBAMA ADMINISTRATION

Regarding the executive action on immigration, after admitting on numerous occasions that it was NOT within his powers to do so, President Obama unilaterally attempted to grant amnesty to more than five million illegal immigrants without the approval of Congress, deliberately not enforcing the current laws on the books that he was, by law, supposed to uphold. Is it not in his oath to support and defend the Constitution against all enemies foreign and domestic, which would include his oath to faithfully execute the laws as passed by Congress?

In eight years, the Obama administration displayed the least professional and worst fiscal accountability of any governing body in American history. "Hyperbole," you say? "Exaggerations and sensationalism," you muse? Look at the facts. We had the highest number of people ever out of the workforce, yet we were told that unemployment was improving, the debt and deficit hit a new record[6], and we had scandals over the IRS, Solyndra, Healthcare.gov, Operation Fast and Furious, Benghazi, Hillary Clinton's emails and uranium transferred to Russia. Furthermore, mountains of cash were awarded to incompetent corporations on the mantra that they were too big to fail. Iran was given pallets of cash, the national debt touched $20 trillion and a Republican Congress continued the debate to raise the debt ceiling—even President Trump reluctantly signed the omnibus bill.

One may think, "That's politics. That's how it goes. So what?" But President Obama did not think that before he took office, nor did many other leftists. Just two years prior to his taking office, then-Senator Obama said:

> *"The fact that we are here today to debate raising America's debt limit is a sign of leadership failure... Increasing America's debt weakens us domestically and internationally. Leadership means that 'the buck stops here'. Instead, Washington is shifting the burden of bad choices today onto the backs of our children and grandchildren. America has a debt problem and a failure of leadership. Americans deserve better."*

Did America understand that "leadership" or the "buck stops here" accountability President Obama spoke of? Negative. Rather, he doubled down on the failed policies of past presidents and nations that managed to drive this country into the ground in less than one term. Sure, President Obama spoke of lofty goals and change, yet he quickly abandoned his principles after taking office. A president that ran on unity effectively divided our nation to a point not seen since the Civil War. A political atrocity such as the Obama administration could only occur in a vacuum of accountability. Now that President Trump is bringing it back, the swamp is fighting to maintain the status quo. The Obama administration got away with these failures because as Americans we do not hold ourselves accountable, we shift blame away from individuals and hold no one or nothing to a standard. That is, until we elected Donald Trump.

Rather than addressing the problem, President Obama and his ilk demonized those who brought these scandals to light. For example, how can we manage government spending if there is no standard, no true debt ceiling? If President Obama was professionally accountable, and Americans held *themselves* accountable, then we could have a standard. The president could have then proposed a way for this country to live within our means. Once again, the lack of accountability and absence of standards led to this disaster.

But why would the American people expect more from the government when our own government officials fail to act responsibly?

CHARLIE WRANGLE

Charlie Wrangle chaired the House Ways and Means Committee from 2007 to 2010. In that powerful position, Wrangle led Congress in determining how to tax the American people, but while taxing you and me, he evaded paying taxes for multiple terms.

Representative Wrangle neglected to report income on rental property he owned in Punta Cana in the Dominican Republic. Furthermore, he never reported that the lender waived the interest on his loan, while other investors paid 10.5 percent. Representative Wrangle reported neither the interest forgiveness nor the rental income until his attorney disclosed publicly that the congressman was in the wrong in light of external oversight.

On top of not reporting his income from his luxurious foreign rental property and sweetheart-deal interest rate, Representative Wrangle never reported the income on the sale of his Washington, DC home, nor did he pay property tax on two of his rental properties in New Jersey. Remember that Representative Wrangle did all this while taxing the American people. He helped make the rules to which we live by, and then he disobeyed them.

When Charlie Wrangle ultimately held himself accountable—or rather when the media and his colleagues actually demanded accountability—the congressman had to report more than half a million dollars of previously unreported income. Ironically, the very man who argued against tax reduction was simultaneously avoiding paying taxes on his assets. The face of the progressive movement rears its head, and this is only the beginning.

Charlie Wrangle was the first congressman to publicly support Occupy Wall Street. Perhaps Occupy Wall Street can overlook Representative Wrangle's Mercedes, numerous onshore and offshore rental properties and his tax evasion, but we cannot. Nor should his constituency. The sad part is that he won his district by 91 percent in 2012 despite all this coming to light, this is the power of propaganda and it can overwhelm reality. Wake up, America. How can we elect people like this? Or people like Hank Johnson from Georgia who actually asked a Navy Admiral during a hearing if they should be concerned that the island of Guam would capsize with the addition of a few thousand troops? Don't believe me? Look it up! This comes from an electorate that simply does not care to investigate who they are putting their vote behind.

ERIC HOLDER AND THE FAST AND FURIOUS SCANDAL

If Congressman Wrangle serves as an example for the woes of our elected officials, let Attorney General Eric Holder stand for the ills of our appointed ones. Eric Holder led the Department of Justice during a major scandal and subsequent cover up.

In Operation Fast and Furious, high-ranking officials, including the Deputy Attorney General, the ATF Director, the FBI Director and top federal prosecutors, planned a sting operation to target high-level firearm smugglers in a tactic known as gun walking. Unfortunately, in this sting operation, the carelessness of the plan led to the death of a border agent and the firearms have subsequently been tracked to numerous violent crimes in the United States and Mexico and to the kingpin Joaquín Archivaldo Guzmán Loera (El Chapo). When the American public discovered their government provided close to $1 million in firearms to Mexican drug cartel smugglers, uproar ensued. The Justice Department and Eric Holder found themselves in the public's crosshairs.

Holder insisted he had no knowledge of the operation. Common sense would dictate, however, that an initiative to track American firearms that involved the heads of the FBI and ATF as well as numerous federal prosecutors and the Deputy Attorney General would have at least popped up on Eric Holder's proverbial radar. Yet Mr. Holder still denied knowledge. Although a Justice Department internal investigation cleared Eric Holder of any involvement in the scandal (of course it did), there were numerous sources claiming he did in fact know, which was exhibited in various emails. Nevertheless, he still never took responsibility for his department's role in the debacle.

What happened to the-buck-stops-here mentality? Why did Eric Holder not just acknowledge the mistake? Why was he not held accountable?

With Wrangle-like hypocrisy, Eric Holder condemned the plan as "fundamentally flawed," yet never admitted his department's actions or role in the scandal. No one was fired, and the department ultimately responsible for prosecuting those criminals targeted in the mission in the first place denied knowledge and condemned the mission. This mentality was echoed in the IRS scandal; Holder has since "resigned," but with no penalty. Where is Holder's account-ability?

BENGHAZI

- Ambassador J. Christopher Stevens and his staff sent multiple requests for added security due to the deteriorating atmosphere in Libya.
- In an act of war, Al Qaida and their affiliates executed a coordinated attack on an American embassy, killing four Americans, including Ambassador Stevens.
- The president, Secretary of State Hillary Clinton and National Security Advisor Susan Rice, among others, lied to the American people on national television for two subsequent weeks calling the attack on the embassy a "spontaneous attack in retaliation for an inappropriate video" made here in the US, despite them knowing that was not the case.
- Admiral Mike Mullen testified to a "hold in place" order given to a nearby Special Operations team.
- Officials are held from public statements and testimonies and forced to sign non-disclosure agreements.

The Obama administration used high-level surrogates to cover an error and, as a result, no one was held accountable, and the individual responsible for making an anti-Islamic video was held in prison as a scapegoat despite First Amendment rights. Secretary Clinton was even quoted saying "what difference does it make," in regard to how or why our citizens were murdered. Yet no one was been fired, repri-manded or jailed. I am not even going in to the fact that she exchanged classified emails on a private server, that her husband (former President Bill Clinton) met with the attorney general who was investigating the matter, that Hillary Clinton smashed laptops and Blackberries with hammers, or that the Clinton Foundation was investigated for fraud.

And she was still was allowed by her party to run for president. Even worse, as a reflection of the morals of our society, she even won the popular vote for president of the United States. America, if you don't think you are susceptible to a false narrative, think again.

IRS

Leading up the 2012 elections, there were allegations of conservative groups, specifically Tea Party groups, being scrutinized and blocked from receiving their nonprofit status, while liberal and progressive groups were far less scrutinized and received the requested status without delay.

The lies to the American people continued after the election. As it became more and more clear that conservative groups were being unfairly targeted, more and more excuses were made, and little responsibility was taken. Two IRS commissioners resigned and Lois Lerner, who became the face of the scandal, lost all of her emails during the questioned time and the IRS couldn't recover them. The IRS requires us to keep our own tax records for seven years, but no punishment is levied for a senior official at that same agency losing official emails? Though Ms. Lerner told the press after the whole ordeal that she was the victim, I think she actually came out ahead in the end. In the couple of the years leading up to her retirement Ms. Lerner received more than $100,000 in bonuses, and when she eventually did retire[7] she received her pension.

President Obama tried to defend the IRS, saying there is "not even a smidgen of corruption" during an interview with Bill O'Reilly. The only investigations have been internal, despite a handful of congressional hearings, which resulted in more bureaucratic red tape. Despite evidence to the contrary, it was pushed off as only a local rogue agent. The agency responsible for executing unbiased regulations regarding our taxes is being used as a political weapon, and it is now in charge of enforcing provisions of our health care system.

HEALTH CARE

As outlined previously, the law destined for the introduction of socialism in America has been a disaster. President Obama promised that "if you like your doctor, you can keep your doctor." This has just been another lie. The law that was to save every American household $2,500 a year, create jobs and be self-sustainable has failed, as proven by the uncovered tapes of Affordable Care Act (ACA) architect Johnathan Gruber calling the American voter "stupid."

This is costing millions of people their current insurance, while only signing up less than half of those through the federal website. The rates and deductibles are too high for the folks who the law was supposed to help in the first place. What is worse is that the Obama administration was counting people who were dropped from their current plans because of the ACA as new enrollees.

The website itself cost the American people hundreds of millions of dollars—just the website! And it still could not effectively sign a single person up on its debut. Kathleen Sebelius, the head of Health and Human Services and the one in charge of the effective role out of the program failed the American people, was allowed to resign with no punishment.

In light of the nearly endless shortcomings of this bill, President Obama, with no authority to do so, changed provisions of the law to make it seem more appealing in the media.

We, as a society, allowed this to happen by continuing to elect those that do not hold true to their offices, oaths and duties. Generation Y, we are doomed to inherit the consequences of this unaccountable government, so it is imperative that we listen up and pull our heads out of the sand.

SOCIETY'S MANDATE

America's lack of accountability is widespread and epidemic, though this is not entirely a generational issue. As the generation who is set to inherit this country's problems, my age group should be the most concerned about the matter. Generation Y must restore itself in order to restore America. The solution is easily stated, but it is truly a vast and demanding task. We must hold ourselves accountable, hold others in society accountable and demand accountability from our government and the media that covers them. To do that we must engage, and we must know history as fact and not as politicians, Hollywood icons or propaganda portray it. Additionally, and most importantly, our generation must become involved in the government —at the local, state and national levels. Only when my generation gains the lion's share of responsibility in government can our collective voice be heard, but what will our message be?

CHAPTER TWO
PATRIOTISM, SACRIFICE
AND SERVICE?

"I like to see a man proud of the place in which he lives. I like to see a man live so that his place will be proud of him."

PRESIDENT ABRAHAM LINCOLN

"We are not going to make America Great Again, it was never that great."

GOVERNOR ANDREW CUOMO

I WOULD JUST LIKE to reflect on Andrew Cuomo's quote before I dive into this topic. He, like Corey Booker, Bernie Sanders, Elizabeth Warren and many others have made a clear effort to degrade this great nation simply because President Trump has made it better. Look at the lengths they were willing to go to destroy Justice Brett Kavanaugh. But Christine Ford, his accuser who had testified under oath that her whole life was destroyed by this man, is no longer pursuing any further course of action. The left has run a campaign of destruction and refused to acknowledge any improvement based on any policy other than those that they control. And if people actually find out that things are better, the Democratic powerbase is afraid that their policies will get them thrown out of office and out of power completely. The left has spent the better part of 2017 and 2018 trying to make America appear as if it is the worst, most racist, unequal, awful place to live. But the truth is that this is the best place in the world to live because even those that scream so loud you can hear them over their pink hair from their parent's basement still don't leave. Unapparelled freedoms, economic opportunity unlike anywhere else, the envy of global achievement—is despised by the left.

America, particularly my generation, has staggering potential but we need to realistically evaluate and correct our weaknesses so that we can improve ourselves and begin to restore the country. Generally, the left is ideologically raised, narcissistic and lacks the patriotic zeal to give back. Proof? What is the percentage of liberals in the military or law enforcement? Military personnel voted for Trump almost 3 to 1. Law enforcement personnel polled for Trump at 84%.[1] What must be paid attention to is that my generation votes Democrat 2:1.[2] Why is this? Because for the most part, we have not endured the same hardships as our parents and grandparents. We do not understand many of the realities of life because our liberal institutions have pulled the wool over our eyes. I will discuss millennials later, but we have been protected from losing and, in some cases, even competing and understanding the sensation of winning. My generation has not seen a world war, a draft, the great depression or factory work at fourteen years old.

To give credit to a Bill Whittle speech: We are the only nation on earth where the primary health concern among poor people is obesity, where even under the poverty line people have iPhones, televisions and air-conditioning. It's no wonder we are voting for the side of government that acts like Santa Clause with other people's money.

In the book, *The Clash of Civilization*, Dr. Samuel Huntingdon pointed to the West's "general weakening of ... 'work ethic' and [the] rise of a cult of personal indulgence."[3] He wrote those words in 1996 and now more than twenty-two years later, the United States has seen a steep increase of narcissism, personal indulgence and apathy.

My generation in particular takes what this country offers for granted. We care little for the heritage and history that has carried the United States and western civilization to greatness. We even criticize or deny certain parts of history. Don't believe me? The next time you have a conversation with a liberal, point out that it was Republicans who freed the slaves without a single vote from the Democrats. You will get "that was a different Republican Party" or something to that effect. Maybe also point out that Democrats exclusively voted for Obamacare and that cost most people more than $1,000, but not a single Democrat voted for President Trump's cut with that put more than $1,000 back in most middle-class people's pockets.

We are partly to blame for not caring to study history but also we were taught not to challenge the school systems that failed us, neglected and sometimes refused to teach history as it happened— they shoulder some of the blame. The very time during our development when we should be exposed to all points of view we were being censored and sheltered to our detriment. Case in point: during the Cold War the US jailed and prosecuted communists and socialists, but now a socialist can run for president and be well received by a large part of the populous. We lack respect for our rights and personal liberties, partly from disregard and partly for the gross lack of education. We don't know the difference between privileges and rights, as the differing views on health care have showed us, and we have no respect for the rights we enjoy and even abuse. Society has endured fewer direct hardships.

We are overly narcissistic. Social media allow us to post our thoughts, feelings and insults under the cloak of anonymity. Everything we do is tracked online, and we expect everyone to care. We voice our grandiose cyberspace contributions with the mask of faceless confrontation, hiding behind a computer screen. We are more obsessed with how many likes we have than we are having a face-to-face dinner conversation with our families.

Why do we feel the world cares if we are *"Christmas shopping—what fun!"*, *"Feeling down, my girlfriend won't return my phone calls,"* *"Making ramen noodles and then watching Honey Boo Boo!"*? We are fighting a global war on terror, people are rioting in the streets because their feelings are state sponsors of terror are testing ICBM's, so does the world really need to know about your *"Trip to the mall with my BFF!"*? Nobody needs to know that. And if you think anyone cares beyond your small group of sheople friends then you're wrong. I'm not saying don't post, share or indulge in social media, but know that, as my profile says; "Twitter is not real life."

This has led to a culture crisis, where people speak out based on headlines and emotions oftentimes without their own due diligence. Even if you have twenty-two followers, sometimes millions will see your post, costing people careers, jobs and families due to public pressure no matter the validity or truth.

Look, I'm speaking to my own, Generation Y. No one cares. If you want the world to care about you, do something of significance. Significance isn't shopping at Forever 21, shot-gunning a beer bong or having your third pumpkin spice latté of the day at Starbucks. Significance is doing something that adds value to our society. Volunteer at a charity, enlist in the armed forces, or start a small business. Do something!

When you add all these flaws together, our generation thinks it is perfectly all right to sit at home on mom's couch and watch reality TV all day. Stop being a drain on the economy and get a job. If you have one, help create more, get educated and help someone other than yourself.

HOW DID WE GET HERE?

I know I have spent the majority of this book telling people to stop blaming others, but you must identify the root of the problem. Who contributed to where we are and how did they do it? We as individuals are not solely responsible because, there are external factors.

1. Ourselves—for allowing apathy, narcissism and indulgence to become the norm.
2. The Baby Boomers—we were taught that we always get a trophy, even for last place. There are winners and losers in the world, in capitalism and t-ball. Get used to it, kids.
3. The media—we were taught to worship worthless celebrities like Miley Cyrus, Lindsay Lohan and the Kardashians. Bruce Jenner was given the ESPY Courage award for thinking he was a woman. Stop putting these clowns in the spotlight and focus on real heroes like business owners, firefighters and the military.
4. Our school system—our history programs are not taught based on American exceptionalism. Our generation was not taught about the personal sacrifices needed to create the United States and western civilization. History classes focused on "downtrodden groups" and "victims of progress." Teach about the founders, the generals, the barons of industry and everyone else who actually shaped America into the superpower it is today.

It is time to take accountability for our actions. Stop Tweeting and posting messages on Facebook all day and forcefully remove your smart phone from your hand. Stop the victim-mentality and earn your right at the top. Get up every day and ask yourself, "What can I do to improve?" Then go do it. Realize that short of curing cancer or defusing a nuclear bomb in Time Square, no one really cares about what you did today. Maybe with your close friends and family you can share that you went to the doctor's office, got mad at your co-worker or bought a new dress, but don't expect recognition from the world. We don't care, but we will when you do something *of* significance.

It is time to educate ourselves where the school system failed. We didn't learn what we needed to in school because our school systems have a leftist agenda. Complain all you want but this is reality. As kids, we could legitimately blame the school system for our inadequacies, but we can no longer because we are adults. Grab a history book and read it. Grab another and read it. Don't stop. You can never know too much history. Knowledge is power and is the very clear reason why some people are so easily manipulated.

It's also about time that we give back. As the former face of national community service, I can say that not enough people serve their communities and that is a grounding experience, even for me. Enlist in the armed forces or seek a commission. Join a charity organization. Start a small business and create a few jobs. Work for something bigger than yourself. Ask others how they made a life for themselves when they grew up. If we join together as a generation and try to build and restore this nation, then we will. But we won't achieve a thing on Facebook.[4]

"My fellow Americans, ask not what your country can do for you, ask what you can do for your country."

JOHN F. KENNEDY

CHAPTER THREE
MULTICULTURALISM

HOW AND WHY WE MUST UNITE AS
AMERICANS, NOT DIVIDE INTO
HYPHENATED AMERICANS

"For the multiculturalist, white Anglo-Saxon Protestants are prohibited, Italians and Irish get a little respect, blacks are good, native Americans are even better. The further away we go, the more they deserve respect. This is a kind of inverted, patronizing respect that puts everyone at a distance."

SLAVOJ ŽIŽEK, AUTHOR, SOCIOLOGIST,
PHILOSOPHER, CULTURAL CRITIC, AND
SELF-DESCRIBED MARXIST

"In the first place, we should insist that if the immigrant who comes here in good faith becomes an American and assimilates himself to us, he shall be treated on an exact equality with everyone else, for it is an outrage to discriminate against any such man because of creed, or birthplace, or origin. But this is predicated upon the person's becoming in every facet an American, and nothing but an American ... There can be no divided allegiance here. Any man who says he is an American, but something else also, isn't an American at all. We have room for but one flag, the American flag ... We have room for but one language here, and that is the English language ... and we have room for but one sole loyalty and that is a loyalty to the American people."

THEODORE ROOSEVELT 1907

AFTER EIGHT YEARS of a president that campaigned on hope and change, he gave many minorities hope for a unified America. He didn't say what hope was, but he told everyone they would have it. President Obama promised that he would fundamentally change America by uniting us. We are now a divided country more than ever and the left did it by reinforcing the current divisions within the groups and cultures that were already there in an effort to have everyone turn to the government to legislate equality. Nothing was solved, in fact, it was made worse. President Trump did not cause this division, he was merely the catalyst injected into a sleeping giant that lay in waiting until the left was out of power. Don't believe me? Look who funds these mob style protests.

Multiculturalism divides our nation into sub-categories, individuals into groups and the individual from his or her individuality. In short, multiculturalism is divisive. Ideally, our nation should resemble a melting pot: peoples from all over the world, coming together in a new land to form a new society, leaving injustices behind and bringing the best of their cultures, not the worst. This is America, the melting pot is an idea where we all share in an American culture that we all create from the BEST parts of the cultures we left behind. There is one culture, comprised of many. Yet leftists attempt to demolish this ideal and replace it with a salad bowl analogy or, even worse, make us feel guilty about our own desires of how culture should be. In their view, there is no American culture. America represents only the vestibule that carries other cultures, and cultures that do not mix, blend or change.

To the left, each cultural group is its own unique segment of society. To those on the right, America itself has a culture where individuals from all walks of life and from all corners of the globe help create it.

Why are there these two philosophical differences? The right places utmost importance on the individual, while the left does so on the collective group. Such a philosophical divide is possible as long as our generation allows the left to use collectivism to control and manipulate the population. The left's philosophy has brought about institutional racism where affirmative action is used to discriminate legally. It has brought about the idea of a black America, a white America, and every color in between. The left's philosophy of multiculturalism has divided America and it needs to end if we are going to put our country back together.

MULTICULTURALISM DIVIDES OUR NATION

The most threatening aspect to multiculturalism is that it divides our country, tearing apart the unity that is America. Dr. Samuel Huntingdon said it best in *Clash of Civilization*, "Historically American national identity has been defined culturally by the heritage of Western civilization and politically by the principles of American Creed on which Americans overwhelmingly agree; liberty, democracy, individualism, equality before the law, constitutionalism and private property. In the late twentieth century both components of American identity have come under concentrated and sustained onslaught from a small but influential number of intellectuals and publicists. In the name of multiculturalism they have attacked the identification of the United States with Western civilization, denied the existence of a common American culture, and promoted racial, ethnic, and other subnational cultural identities and groupings."[1]

Contrary to what the left believes, we are not a group of sub-nationals bound together by geography. We are one nation bound together by a common belief in American values, liberty, democracy, individualism, constitutionalism, Judeo-Christian morals and free trade. We are not a salad bowl, but a melting pot of all the greatness the world has to offer, rejecting all things that do not support this common belief. We take the best of the world and make it our own. And most importantly, we all share in that greatness as *Americans*.

The multiculturalism of the left seeks to deny American culture and rather insist that America is merely a collection of other cultures. This concept divides us because it refuses to recognize the common bond of Americanism that we all share. Where does this concept end? Do we allow pockets of home-rule groups, like we do with the Native American reservations? Do we allow immigrant groups to enforce their own laws and have their own court system? Some leftists believe that Muslim immigrants should be allowed to continue to follow Sharia law, despite the obvious conflict with American values and law—as well as the Constitution.

I do not consider myself a European who happens to live in America. I am a flag-waving, meat-eating, single-gender American and that is not a bad thing despite your personal beliefs.

MULTICULTURALISM DIVIDES OUR SOCIETY

Multiculturalism is dangerous because it divides society into subcategories and groups. Why do we hear pundits speak of winning the Latino vote, the women vote or the black vote? Because previous generations have allowed the left to convince us that our society is divided into ethnic groups and at times even given preferential treatment.

Theodore Roosevelt and Barack Obama both made statements that there is not a "black America" or a "white America" or "fifty-fifty Americans," such as German-Americans, but rather only Americans. I am ethnically European but do not consider myself European-American. Again, I am an American and proud of it!

The left is quick to celebrate every ethnic difference and nuance because with each difference, with each divide, American identity and culture grow weaker. The left has recently put diversity ahead of qualifications; liberal representatives across government and pop culture embrace division and it has cost them big time, yet they still don't look in the mirror to examine why they lost so big in 2016.

During my tours in Iraq I noted how their cultures are divided into Sunni, Shiite and Kurd. They lack any notion of an Iraqi nationalism. To them the idea of national unity is lost. Their divide weakens their country, leads to instability that can only be controlled by a dictator like Saddam Hussein and explains why they will never adopt our Jeffersonian democracy. They are only united by Islam, breeding many with a hatred for western civilization. It turns my stomach when I see the left attempting to divide our country into blocks like those so common in Iraq, maybe not by religious faction but by race, ideology and socioeconomic status.

While serving in the military, I engaged with a fellow service member that happened to be black. The service member insisted he was African-American and felt that calling himself anything but that would discredit his heritage. When asked, he could not point to any specific ancestors that came from Africa, dating as far back as his great grandparents. In addition, neither he nor his parents had ever so much as traveled to Africa and had no know descendants still living there. I explained that this makes him American, just like me, and that's okay. In fact, it is a good thing because that's what we shared, what we signed up to defend and what represented the strength of the military brotherhood. Despite my attempt to explain to him our unity and common love for America, he told me I was no brother of his. I was subsequently counseled for being insensitive by my superiors. I then asked if I could be called Middle Eastern-American, because presumably that is the cradle of civilization. My senior chief's response was "Carl that is ridiculous. You have no decedents from there nor honor any of their heritage," to which my reply was, "Exactly, should we not be telling my fellow service member the same thing under that premise?" This is the fundamental problem with sub-groups, you must treat them all differently.

Just as I do not identify as European-American, neither should anyone in our generation. Even those who immigrated to America are Americans. As Theodore Roosevelt said, "There can be no fifty-fifty Americanism in this country. There is room here for only 100 percent Americanism, only for those who are American and nothing else."

MULTICULTURALISM DIVIDES AN INDIVIDUAL FROM HIS OR HER INDIVIDUALITY

Worse yet is that multiculturalism robs individuals of their individuality. If a child is told their entire life that they are an "X"-American, if they fill out that they are an "X"-American on every application, and if they are told that "X"-Americans are somehow different than other Americans, then that child will associate them self with being an "X"-American. The "X"-American will become their identity. They will believe that they must act as an "X"-American, hold the beliefs of "normal" "X"-Americans, and that he or she (yes, one of two genders) is somehow different by birth than other Americans, because after all he or she is an "X"-American.

I blame affirmative action for this particular kind of social wrong. Affirmative action treats individuals differently on the basis of race, ethnicity and gender. This is blatant discrimination. It forces multiculturalism on society in a way that does far more damage than the salad bowl myth.

Caucasians resent affirmative action because it penalizes us for being white. Non-Caucasians should resent it because affirmative action treats them differently solely on race and not merit. Worse yet, many view minorities who have obtained high levels of success with a sense of suspicion that the individual may not have risen so high without affirmative action policies.[2] Once again, multiculturalism strips the individual of individuality.

On the other hand, the left has tried to strip physical descriptions from use in profiling, as we saw in the Trayvon Martin incident in Florida. Law enforcement was chastised for identifying Trayvon Martin as black, and there was a subsequent media storm that race should no longer be used to describe suspects because it makes them biased. Statistically, (not my opinion, so relax CNN) black people per capita commit more crime than some other races but identifying a suspect as black may lead officers to make assumptions based on a stereotype and that could hurt someone's feelings in a criminal pursuit. Sounds dumb, huh? But instead of working toward a solution, the left throws this in the face of anyone who dares to challenge the liberal mantra, screaming institutional racism.

Here is where I have landed myself in trouble before, but I see no reason to stop now. According to the same group that seeks to divide, it is also in some way racist to even discuss this matter. Because I may derive an opinion different from theirs related to anything about race, religion or creed, I am somehow the one who is racist. The left has overplayed this because people (specifically Republicans) are sick of being called racists for exercising a freedom of thought derived from fact. In fact, this is exactly why Donald Trump won in 2016 because he said enough. The left has never hated anyone more, or accused anyone of more racism, than Donald Trump. Yet going into the 2018 midterms his approval rating from black voters is three times higher than any other Republican in recent history. The left has sought to discourage anyone from challenging their narrative by publicly screaming "Racist!" The problem is that they have weaponized racism so much that when actual racism occurs, it is not regarded as it should be and creates a disadvantage to those that are *actually* experiencing it.

WHAT DO YOU DO?

The solution here is more complex than just those offered in this book because things like multiculturalism and affirmative action are culturally ingrained into our society and if one were to propose getting rid of it and going to a true merit-based system... you guessed it, they would be called a racist. The solution must come mostly from society, but government can still offer solutions by literally doing less.

Despite the obvious immediate fallout, we need candidates that are willing to take on the issue of abolishing preferential treatment on the basis of race, ethnicity, gender, color, creed or sexual orientation.[3] Do away with questions pertaining to these qualities on all federal applications, paperwork and so forth.

Holidays that celebrate on the basis of race, ethnicity, sexual preference, creed and any division of the like are only drawing more division. Why do we have Pacific Islander Heritage Month? If you ask, "But how will we ever learn about the achievements of certain groups?" This is easy: teach history, as it happened, in school, and the problem is solved. If the Pacific Islander group did anything significant, an actual history class will reflect that, but do not manufacture significance for the sake of diversity.

America as a culture, the product of numerous cultures, needs to be encouraged. For example, when someone asks about your heritage, anticipating that you'll say Italian or Mexican, reply, "I'm American, but my ancestors came from... [fill in the blank]."

As for affirmative action, completely do away with it at all levels. How can we reward one group for being black, Latino, and so forth without implicitly punishing another group for being Asian, Indian, white, etc.? End affirmative action, which is state-based discrimination and the only true institutionalized racism left in America, and return to a true meritocracy. No more organizations for black engineers, Hispanic lawyers and the like. If private foundations want scholarships based on race, they are free to do that independent of government assistance. I even encourage that. We are a nation built from individuals. We must reward individuals rather than groups. We must encourage productivity and free thought, not collectivism.

Many will and have considered me a bigot for holding such beliefs that all Americans are *American* but take a step back and look at my plan before reacting. The irony is that the people screaming the loudest about bigotry are the ones that refuse to accept any views but their own. I simply want equal treatment for all and a merit-based society where one's work and talents earn rewards, not color and ethnicity.

CHAPTER FOUR
MILLENNIALS...WHAT
HAPPENED TO US

OVER THE LAST two decades we have seen a division of this country along political lines not seen since the Civil War. It has been driven by the ease of dissemination of information, or misinformation through conventional and social media. This is propaganda. When most people hear that word they scream conspiracy and think of North Korea. Propaganda, defined by Merriam-Webster, is "ideas, facts, or allegations spread deliberately to further one's cause or to damage an opposing cause; also: a public action having such an effect."

It is not a militant term forced on people; it is simply any message made public to further an agenda. And if you don't think you are affected by it, then think again.

Generations have been affected differently, but at the heart of this impact are millennials, drinking information at the flow rate of a fire hose, unable to turn it off even if desired. We are the most affected and we have become the most engaged for better and worse. We are the Americans born in the eighties and nineties. We comprise 30 percent of the American population and represent the cutting edge in today's workforce.

Due to the ease of the ability to seek recognition, we have, in large part, defined ourselves as self-consumed, entitled and those who think we know everything and deserve the same. Companies rewrite policies to accommodate our generation's appalling behavior out of a lack of understanding of our pompous attitude. We think we deserve every job, and after we get it we have the same moral authority to disobey our superiors because, of course, we know better. This stems from little league, gym class and other social programs where the merit of our achievement was secondary to our attendance. This has led to many of us who live with our parents long after college while we figure out what we want to do, waiting for a perfect job instead of taking one now and building our résumé. And why? Because we have been fed propaganda teaching us that this was acceptable, catered to by the success of our previous generations.

In life not everyone is a winner. Losers are not rewarded, winners are. Our parents hid this axiom from us, with the best intentions, turning us into excuse-making, attention-craving two-faced monsters.[1] Nothing was ever our fault, and our ability to hold ourselves accountable has suffered. We cannot handle rejection, loss, criticism or deprivation of any sort, and we are almost a ruined generation because of it. Frighteningly, the generation that pawns accountability on others will soon inherit the nation's responsibilities. Will we cower in fear? Will we hide behind our computers, in the shadows of the anonymity of our blogs and social media? Will our lack of responsibility cause us to make excuses? Will it cause us to fail in our inherited mission to save or even maintain the republic that afforded the privileges we enjoy? America deserves better, so it's time that we as a generation get our acts together, get involved and stop making excuses.

George Washington Carver said, "Ninety-nine percent of the failures come from people who have the habit of making excuses." Could you imagine if our founding fathers sat around whining about the British taxes on the colonies? We could still be under British rule. If President Roosevelt had sat and cried about Pearl Harbor instead of declaring war, we might be speaking Japanese or even German. Imagine if almost 50 percent of Americans didn't work and needed the money from those that did work to live.... Oh, wait that is happening now because they have been spoon-fed a narrative of victimhood.

If you fail or come upon a hard time, make reasonable assessments to attempt to correct and overcome the issue or issues. Don't whine, complain or shift blame. Certainly don't think you are entitled to have others take care of you. If you're faced with a difficult decision, choose the honorable and moral path. If you make a mistake, learn from it and see to it that you never repeat it. It's all about personal accountability, and the lack of it in our generation has created a lot of problems for the country. Failure is okay as long as you learn from it. The best boxers will say it's not how hard you can hit, it's how hard you can get hit and get back up, but that is not what we are being taught now.

We are a generation torn between big government Democrats, wavering Republicans and a new class of emerging "reality" politicians. We are seeing this rise from pop culture and military veterans, many with liberal social policies and conservative constitutional values. We have seen both sides of what causes us to prosper and fail and we are arguably the smartest yet the laziest generation to date. We grew up with a household computer and video games, and we live by social media platforms that we invented. We have seen the internet boom, the real estate bubble, the 9/11 terror attacks and two major wars, and all before most of us graduated from college.

And yet we still lack many of the fundamental common knowledge and common decency of previous generations: jump starting a car, looking someone in the eye when you shake hands, starting a fire or basic economics. We embrace free speech unless we don't agree with it, preach about acceptance unless it offends us and champion free college and health care without an understanding of how they will be funded. This is caused by how we have been raised, by the need for instant gratification, an excuse orientation and the absence of individual responsibility.

We differ from our elders in the desire to serve. So many of us become content and under achieve within our personal lives and career aspirations because we were used to receiving a trophy for everything. Fewer believe in civil duties, responsibilities and charity than our parents' generation. Many of us argue that government should not interfere with our personal lives or our freedoms, but then complain that the government doesn't do enough and whine for the government to take care of us. Why can't we start taking action to fix our problems without the government's help? Why is our generation trading our freedoms for short-term gain as big government passes constitutional and social infringements? When you see adult liberal Democrats take place in a sit-in to try to further gun control in a building protected by guns, how are we not outraged at the hypocrisy? Instead our generation cheers for it.

Most of us don't understand wasteful government spending, gigantic deficits and a colossal national debt. Now as we enter the workforce and begin to own our first homes, we are realizing the reality that these inherited monsters will eventually creep out from under our beds as we saw in the 2008 crash. As a result, many of us entering the workforce see the effects of some of the policies our institutions taught us to cheer for in the deductions category on our paystubs. This has bred a transformation, a new political class of socially liberal and fiscally conservative, which is not accepted by the establishment of either party, so we are torn between voting with our hearts and our brain. We are beginning to understand the blunders of preceding generations that will fall on us at a time when we are expected to financially support the Baby Boomers as they collect Social Security and Medicare. We know that we must make changes, but not ones that affect us. We will inherit this burden unprepared. We are waking up slowly, but will it be too late?

While I believe we are turning a corner for the better, in light of the epic failure of President Obama and his liberal policies, I think our generation at times can be ignorant and blind to the long-term consequences of our immediate actions. Our problems largely stem from our generation's lack of concern, our self-indulgence, general apathy and failure to learn from history. We are more than happy to call out our generation's flaws, but we do not admit our own. In true Carl Higbie fashion, I call it as I see it because I am more worried about who is affected rather than who is offended.

I know we inherited many challenges, some we were taught to ignore, and we know it is our mandate to rise to those challenges. We understand that if we as a nation are to survive, we must change our current path. We must respect the sanctity of our institutions while at the same time use them as vehicles of change. As one of the few senior millennial presidential appointees in the Trump administration, I saw this firsthand. Most, even non-millennials, complained about the way things were run yet many never had the authority or desire to actually effect change. But that never stopped the bitching.

We must understand that groups like Occupy Wall Street, largely supported by the institutional left machine, are using my generation as their puppets, where many government handout recipients destroyed business in protest of capitalism, decrying any success not evenly distributed. Don't believe me? Just watch Austen Fletcher's YouTube videos; he confronts these protestors who rarely have actual jobs and are literally paid to protest.

As we reflect once we have left the sheltered views of our liberal institutions, many of which pay people like Elizabeth Warren with eight-digit personal wealth and $400,000 salaries to simultaneously denounce the pay structure of Wall Street with comparable salaries. Imagine the irony: those people on Wall Street who are successful work twelve to sixteen-hour days, innovate and actually produce a tangible product where those making those salaries in universities are subsidized by either tax payer money or back-breaking student loans to those who attend these institutions. And for what, degrees in gender studies, philosophy or art? Most people who enter the private sector will attest how little what they are taught in college applies to the jobs they enter, outside of trades or specialty degrees. We see the hypocrisy yet have trouble recognizing the effect of the propaganda machine.

Our teachers and the institutional establishments unequally bombarded us with liberal propaganda while we progressed through the public school systems. My classmates and I were required to read "Weekly Readers" in elementary school that warned of global warming and an assortment of cause célèbre of the time as fact rather than opinion. We wonder only in retrospect why teachers required us to write papers about presidents such as Lyndon B. Johnson, Woodrow Wilson and Bill Clinton, but rarely Ronald Reagan or George H. W. Bush.

We then went to universities and colleges that were dominated by liberal bias. It was expected that all of our professors would be left leaning, and we were expected to play to their bias to ensure a good grade in the class, never to unleash free thought. If you were not a liberal on a college campus you were considered an outsider, and your political affiliation could even affect your grades. In the single most important time in our lives to learn how to think freely, we were bombarded by an agenda and, for the most part, graded on our acceptance of it first and our performance second.

When Muslim terrorists attacked our nation on 9/11, our generation had no choice but to look to the outside world and to reflect on our government, our foreign policy and the standing of the United States in the world. George W. Bush's "We will not falter" speech immediately united us with patriotic passion only to have our society turn on the very war we supported in the first place. Our generation is political because the media, school system and our enemies abroad have forced us to be. When reality comes knocking, we challenge our institutions with facts while the institutions battle back with emotions, often winning our hearts and overruling our brains.

As our generation assumes more leadership positions in the government, military and private sector, how should we proceed? What changes must we make? How will we define ourselves and the nation we inherited? Do we want to let the America we grew up in slip away, or will we wise up and fight to save our nation?

Historically, each generation of Americans—from our founding fathers who freed us from British tyranny, to those who struggled to define our nation during the Civil War, to the greatest generation that survived the Great Depression and won the Second World War —was forced to make a stand and unite against those who took our liberties away, not each other. Generation Y is no different.

Facing what some call the Great Recession, two of our nation's longest wars, a changing geopolitical world map that is witnessing the nationalist movement of Trump, Brexit, Europe's steady decline due to many of the same policies the left is implementing here, continued unrest in Africa, Asia and the Middle East, and the rise of new powers such as the Russia, China, North Korea, Radical Islam, ISIS, and the Muslim Brotherhood, our generation must understand these for what they are, no matter how inconvenient the truth, not how they are perceived by the progressives and main stream media and certainly not what is easy or politically correct to accept. We must react to these changes and secure America's leading position in the world. With the shortcomings of the Obama Administration, the sleeping economic time bombs of Social Security and other entitlement programs, and with a Constitution that even the Supreme Court occasionally disassembles, like what we saw with President Trump's first immigration order struck down by the 9th Circuit Court, a court that has nearly 80 percent of its rulings overturned by the US Supreme Court, we are in an ideological civil war.

How did we get here? As I progressed through early adulthood—spending much of that time as a United States Navy SEAL fighting in the Middle East and traveling to dozens of countries, I quickly learned that our elder generation could not always be counted on. We watched as politicians, military leaders and business executives traded the responsibility of the stewardship of America for short-term, quick, cheap and selfish gains. Bluntly stated, we have seen too often how those in the establishment have put their own needs ahead of the needs of our nation. Yet every time Baby Boomers shirk their inherited responsibility to maintain American greatness, our generation suffers, and America is further diminished and edging ever closer to the point of no return.

The exact experience that prompted me to begin writing this book and motivated my conviction was my experience in government in the Trump administration. Upon my appointment as the chief of external affairs of the Corporation for National and Community Service, one of three of the highest-ranking appointees there at the time, I was told by career bureaucrats and our general counsel (an appointee) to sit back for two years and let them run the place, to essentially put this experience on my résumé and move on. Work was not rewarded, but complacency was. Had I kept my head down and not tried to actually reform the agency to fit the Trump administration's agenda, I would not have been attacked in the media, which led to my resignation. A victim of my own integrity, I was the subject of a media onslaught by CNN.

This is what we face on the political left: an elitist view espousing to be morally higher, accepting and tolerant unless you disagree, in which case your views have no morals, are deemed racist and intolerant. This is the weapon of choice to keep opposing views at bay, even when they are based on facts.

Our generation must make a stand against those who value political correctness above all else, against myopic politicians and nonsense spewing college professors, and against the mainstream media. We inherited this land from our founding fathers and every generation that came after those great men. Now it is our time, because it is our country and our responsibility to steward this nation. We have an inherited mandate to restore this nation and bring America back to greatness—before it's too late.

PART THREE

FISCAL RESPONSIBILITY

"Too often in recent history liberal governments have been wrecked on rocks of loose fiscal policy."

PRESIDENT FRANKLIN D. ROOSEVELT

CHAPTER FIVE
FEDERAL WELFARE

WHAT DO THE "NEEDY" REALLY NEED AND ENTITLEMENT PROGRAMS HOLDING OUR ECONOMY HOSTAGE

UNTIL THE CIVIL WAR, a group of people designated by a specific skin color were forced to provide a steady stream of labor as slaves. Now a group designated by economic class is given food and housing for a steady stream of votes. The government, mostly brought to us by those on the left, is enslaving people by keeping them dependent on these handouts. The irony is almost unbearable. Has slavery really ended, or are leftist elites enslaving an economic class without them even knowing it, conning an entire economic class into voting for them while they promise them other people's hard-earned resources?

People in this country, and I say people and not Americans because even illegal immigrants can get their hands on these benefits, can seek assistance from the government for food, housing, energy, health care, education, work, insurance, retirement and tax breaks. In 2014 about two thirds of the federal budget was spent on entitlement programs, including Social Security, Medicare, Medicaid and other welfare programs, according to the Heritage Foundation[1].

The Supplemental Nutrition Assistance Program (SNAP), Woman, Infants and Children Nutrition Program (WIC), Temporary Assistance for Needy Families (TANF), Low Income Home Energy Assistance Program (LIHEAP), The Emergency Food Assistance Program (TEFAP), Tax Credit Assistance Programs, Federal TRIO Programs, Home Investment Partnerships Program (HIME), Housing Opportunities for Persons with AIDS (HOPWA), Indian Housing Block Grants, Rural Education Achievement Program, School Breakfast Program, Supplemental Security Income, Additional Child Tax Credit and Transitional Cash and Medical Services for Refugees are just some of the means-tested welfare programs provided by our government and are available to the "needy." Our generation has most likely never heard of most of most of these programs, but that doesn't mean we aren't paying for them and will continue to pay more than any previous generation as our debt grows to a record high. This seems like a pretty long list, but the total list of these programs is much longer.

The US is different than most countries in the fact that the poor do not necessarily need to turn to the government for help. The private sector also offers programs for the less fortunate in the form of volunteered charity contributions and labor. Local food shelves, Goodwill and the Salvation Army are all well-known charities that help the poor in the United States. I know this because I was the face of the Corporation for National and Community Service. I saw these programs firsthand in almost every state across America. Though it is true that most of these private organizations receive some government funding from agencies like CNCS, these organizations also have solid operating plans that enable them to survive and continue to help people if the tax payers weren't forced to pay for it, while government welfare programs do not.

So, it is just not true that the taxpayers have to foot the bill for government welfare programs or risk poor people dying in the streets. This is just what the left wants us to believe. They are scared that if the majority of Americans find out they can get the same services or better from the private sector, which is true most of the time, then the government would lose much of their power, and the Democrats would lose their voter base.

Politicians have used the racial statistic of blacks per capita on welfare to generalize and politicize the welfare issue for decades, calling Republicans racists for wanting to cut programs. Of course, the Democrats are a large part of what keeps these welfare programs alive, and people aren't going to slap away the hand that feeds them. It's no wonder that they historically vote Democrat, and Democrats know that. This is one of the reasons why Democrats want to keep black people in poverty because that ensures them a polarizing talking point and the black vote. But the black community is no longer being played, with social icons coming out in support of Donald Trump, telling their communities to stop buying the crap the left is selling. President Trump's approval in the black community shot to 36 percent. On the other hand, during the 2018 State of the Union speech not a SINGLE member of the Congressional Black Caucus stood to applaud when the President said that "African-American unemployment is at an all-time low." That, ladies and gentlemen is the Democratic Party—upset that President Trump is empowering people.

During his war on poverty, President Johnson said far worse, simply said what many Democrats think even now. Wake up, America. This is your compassionate left showing their true colors and the more they lose, the further they go. Conservatives don't support spending on these welfare programs, not because we want these people to live in poverty, but because we know that without these programs people will be incentivized to live better, liberty-filled lives. I for one believe suffering breeds motivation, a principal that kept me alive during war and led to achievement in the private sector.

"The US has the third highest level of per capita government social welfare spending. This is striking given that government spending is more tightly targeted on the poor and elderly in the US" according to Robert Rector from the Heritage Institute in a September 2015 study.[2] Rector explored what poverty is really like in the United States, and what he found is shocking.

When counting private contributions toward the amount of money spent on social welfare in the US, the spending per capita is almost twice what the average is in Europe, according to Rector. The only other country who spends more than the US per person is Norway. If welfare spending in the US is higher than socialist style countries in Europe, we have a major problem. I think this also shows that it is safe to say that the poor in this country are getting more than a fair share of help.

If you disagree consider this: in 2014 a family of four was considered to be living in poverty if the household income was less than $24,008 a year. The value of the benefits the family received in food, housing, tax credits, energy and education was not counted towards this amount, and the amount spent by the government on these benefits was largely not considered when the Census Bureau calculated the poverty income threshold, according to the same study by Robert Rector.

Let me be clear I am not against helping the poor and less fortunate, I actually did it for a living, I am simply against spending other people's money so subsidize non-essentials like iPhones and flat screen televisions. If a family of four does not have to pay, or is paying very little, for food, housing, and energy, and is getting a tax break—then on top of that is earning $24,000 per year—they are no longer just getting by, they are living better than the bulk of our military personnel whose averages pay is about $40,000 a year (keep in mind they volunteered to possibly die for our country). It is time for our generation to reevaluate who really needs help in this country, to stop voting with our hearts and to start voting with our heads.

In my mind the people who need government help are those who truly cannot survive without the extra assistance. Just because someone is poor does not necessarily mean they *need* government help. If a family is able to afford food and a roof over their heads, then they do not need assistance. If you have everything you absolutely need, and just can't afford something you want, too bad. Americans are starting to forget that we are not entitled to anything except those rights in our Constitution. Look how many people think health care is a right.

According to government reports, Mr. Rector found that people who were actually considered to be living in poverty and were receiving government benefits have a lot more than they need. Of the poor households in America, at least half or over half have air conditioning, cable or satellite television, and a personal computer, and over half of families with kids have a gaming system. Also, around 40 percent have internet and a wide screen plasma television, while 25 percent have a digital video recorder. The worst part about this is these numbers came from government reports, which means the government is fully aware of the fact that these people own these things and still provide substantial aid.

And on top of everything, 42 percent households considered to be living in poverty occupy three-bedroom homes with garages and porches. Though this sounds like a nice place to live, it is clearly more than just getting by.

It is pretty ironic that the left is always talking about how everything needs to be fair, but you never hear them complain about how unfair it is that the government steals hardworking Americans' money and gives it to people who don't contribute. Tell me, is it fair that a middle-class family decides to spend their money only on things that they need so they don't have to go on government assistance, but the government just takes their money anyway, in many cases, to give it to people who decided that they would rather spend their money on an Xbox or second computer instead of food or a house?

And if the money spent by the government to assist the poor was all of a sudden gone, or at least severely decreased, there would not be millions of people living in the streets dying of hunger. In fact, there would be very few if any. According to the United States Department of Agriculture in 2009, Mr. Rector found that 96 percent of parents who are considered poor said their kids have never gone hungry because they couldn't afford food. Also, of the total people considered poor, only 4 percent have been homeless temporarily in the last year. Not bad considering that in 2009 nearly 75,000 veterans were homeless, according to the Population Reference Bureau.[3]

I understand the fact that most people in America have never gone hungry and are able to lead a life where they can come home to their three-bedroom, air-conditioned house and play video games with their kids regardless of their social status. Overall, this is a good thing and is something we should strive for, but the way that it is done is wrong. Our generation has become accustomed to this lifestyle, and we are overwhelmingly failing to recognize that these benefits are funded by the sacrifice of others. For almost every person in poverty who gets government assistance, someone else had to work an extra few hours and be away from their family so they could afford to pay their bills and the taxes.

If our we truly want to see up close how government welfare is abused by those who are on it, we should be cashiers at grocery stores. In high school many of my friends worked as cashiers at local grocery stores. Almost every shift they would see someone buy cigarettes and booze with cash and then buy their food with food stamps. Even worse, some people would buy a few hundred dollars' worth of lottery tickets in cash, then come back and buy junk food with food stamps.

"The US should not seek to outspend other nations in its anti-poverty programs. Instead, the US should seek to reduce poverty by promoting self-sufficiency: the ability to support one's self and family above the poverty level without reliance on welfare aid," Mr. Rector said. "The key to improving self-sufficiency is to increase work and healthy marriage. Increased self-reliance will lead to an enhanced sense of self-achievement, a principal component of human well-being. Restoring healthy marriage will sharply reduce poverty, improve child outcomes, and increase adult happiness."

And just like that, we are back to the solution of many of our problems, and that is that Americans need to start taking responsibility for their actions and for themselves. Government spending on welfare has continued to grow for decades with no sign of long-lasting decreases. This out-of-control spending can't exactly be blamed on just one party, because historically both have contributed to it.

According to *Forbes* contributor Mike Patton, overall spending on welfare since John F. Kennedy has greatly increased, regardless of which party is in charge.[4] Since 1960 the total percent increase in welfare spending when Democrats have been in control of congress is 13.7 percent, with a 3.5 percent increase when Republicans were in control.

The sad reality of this is that both parties ultimately increased spending on welfare. It doesn't really matter that the Republicans didn't increase the spending as much as the Democrats, there was still an increase rather than a decrease, and this is something that a country that is over $20 trillion in debt really can't afford. As my generation begins to reach ages when we can hold public office, we must understand this detriment.

Electing politicians who will promise to cut welfare spending, or at least not increase it, is a start. But let's be honest, even while Ronald Reagan was in office welfare spending increased by 4.3 percent, and while the Republicans were in control of Congress during Bill Clinton's administration, welfare spending was increased by 2.5 percent. If history shows anything, it doesn't matter who you elect, spending on welfare will ultimately increase. Why? Because Democrats are winning that war, they are buying votes with the promise of benefits.

Our nation can survive a Barack Obama, what we cannot survive is a population willing to continue to elect people who make the same promises as him over and over again. History proves that no matter who is in office, welfare spending is not likely to decrease. As always, the government is not the solution to our problem, it is the people. What is needed is a serious culture change; if we do not alter our course, the system may collapse.

In America's current culture people think it is acceptable to spend beyond their means. Being fiscally responsible is not a priority but having the coolest new gadget, no matter the cost, is. If two people are not married and barely have enough money to take care of themselves, is it fair to bring a baby into the world under those conditions?

A culture that lacks responsibility and a hard work ethic will fail. It is time we bring back fiscal and social responsibility to our culture. Only when people start promoting a culture where people are expected to be responsible for themselves and their actions will we begin to see a decrease of those on government welfare.

CHAPTER SIX
OBAMA'S HEALTH CARE
DISASTER

A PRIVILEGE, NOT A RIGHT

"I might be in favor of national health care if it required all Democrats to get their heads examined."

ANN COULTER

"Mr. President, the buzz saw that your health care bill ran into wasn't lobbyists and special interests it was tens of millions of Americans who were saying, 'Stop!'"

JOHN BOEHNER

HEALTH CARE IS NOT A RIGHT, it is a privilege earned by your personal priorities, employment and financial capability. It is wrong, stupid and constitutionally illegal to mandate anyone to purchase anything. It has been proven that programs such as this crush medical innovation and advancements. Why do you think that so many wealthy people from countries like Canada and Great Britain who have these socialized programs flock to America for advanced medical procedures?

Nowhere in the US Constitution does it say that health care is a right, but everyone seems to be ignoring this. Democrats know this, but they have convinced a large section of the electorate that it is to can gain more power. Similar to their promise of welfare programs, the Democrats offer of free health care is all about securing votes. Remember, the more you have to rely on the government the more power they have.

In 2015 the Supreme Court helped increase the government's power when it ruled that government subsidies for health care to Americans nationwide under the Affordable Care Act (ACA) were constitutional. This decision forces Americans who can afford health care to pay for those who can't. It seems like a nice idea, helping those who can't, or really won't, help themselves, but what happens when there are more people who can't afford it than can? The argument in support of this Medicare expansion is what works for thirty to forty million people now should be able to work for twenty, thirty, forty or one hundred million. It will break the system! What happens when someone, who could previously afford health care when they were just paying for themselves, cannot shoulder the extra costs of others' health care and fall into poverty? What happens is the American people lose and the government wins.

There already is a health care system run by the government called the Veterans Health Administration. The Department of Veterans Affairs has failed miserably at providing health care to the very people that have risked their lives for this country, and for some reason the American public think they will miraculously get it right for everyone else. Yeah, fat chance.

The really tricky part is that there are two parts of our health care system: actual health care and health care insurance. The ACA did nothing to address the actual cost of health care but rather further regulated just the cost of insurance. Nationally, the cost of an aspirin in an emergency department can range from a few cents to over $30, a visit to the ER can set you back a few hundred dollars to $17,000, and an ambulance ride can cost $6,500.[1] Hospitals know that with a government mandate for insurance, that the insurers will pay! These were all concerns of the critics of the bill, yet it was passed with zero Republican support.

The ACA was signed into law in March 2010, and in October 2013 Americans were able to enroll in a health care plan. The new plans went into effect in January 2014. According to a 2009 Gallup poll, before Obamacare was signed into law, "80 percent (of Americans) were satisfied with the quality of medical care available to them," while only 38 percent cited cost being an issue.[2] In 2015, over a year after Obamacare was enacted, only 67 percent of Americans were satisfied with their health care.[3] Shocker right? Not for most.

One thing that is hidden to the public is the actual number of Americans that Obamacare applied to. Sure, liberal pundits touted 20 million people insured, but how many lost their current plans? Total estimates say that less than 6 million people actually received new care—less than 2% of America actually used Obamacare. So why was it such a big rattle to the health care system? Because it gave the left massive regulatory control over all health insurance, even for those not covered under Obamacare. For example, men were forced to have mammogram and pregnancy related insurance.

But how have we bamboozled the American public into this? Enter the individual mandate. As one of the architects of Obamacare said, "the stupidity of the American people" allowed it to be rammed down our throats with a law mandating participation. Ironically the progressives then cheered about how many people signed up, never mind that fact that it was now a law. Without the individual mandate, the system doesn't work. Because they need healthy people to pay for sick people. Without the mandate, healthy folks don't sign up and the only people who do sign up are the ones needing expensive care.

Now that President Trump has scrapped the mandate with his new tax reform, the system is failing fast. Insurance companies are facing the reality of risky plans for high-cost individuals and, as capitalism does, dropping out of markets that are not profitable or raising their premiums. While this is bad for some, increased premiums are good for most. Here is why: healthy people who were being forced to pay for the sick now have drastically lower premiums if they *choose* to purchase health care, where the clients that actually consume the greatest resources of health care are now saddled with their own bills.

"Americans who get their health insurance through government-sponsored or assisted plans, such as Medicare and Medicaid or veterans' insurance, are most likely to be satisfied with the way the health care system is working for them than those who have employer-paid insurance or who pay for insurance themselves," Rebecca Riffkin said based on the findings of the poll.

Ms. Riffkin admits that, "Americans' satisfaction appears to be influenced by the nature of their health plans, particularly how much they have to contribute to the cost."

So, people who get their health care for free are more satisfied than those who have to pay for it themselves... Shocker. Let me remind America again that the government does not create anything, all of the money it spends must be confiscated from those who do produce.

The prices for those who are supporting themselves, either through purchasing their own health care or their employers' health care plans, have increased. According to the Kaiser Family Foundation[4], "in 2015, the average annual premiums for employer-sponsored health insurance are $6,251 for single coverage and $17,545 for family coverage. Each rose 4 percent over the 2014 average premiums." This increase effects almost 150 million people.

According to a similar survey by the foundation, "in 2009 the average annual premiums for employer-sponsored health insurance are $4,824 for single coverage and $13,375 for family coverage." From 2005 to 2015 total average annual health insurance premiums have increased by 61 percent and the amount that workers contribute increased by 83 percent.

Americans are not saving money on their new health care plans, and even those who don't pay for their health care directly are paying for it in taxes and through the loss of their freedom of choice in their doctors and health care plans. And on top of everything they are still less satisfied with it. But the left was prepared to counter these concerns in case the people figured this out.

"It's about jobs. In its life (health care reform) will create 4 million jobs, 400,000 jobs almost immediately," Nancy Pelosi said in 2010.[5]

So where are the jobs? Obamacare has and will continue to cost jobs because the increased cost to employer's premiums outside the health industry will force them to lay off workers. This national health care plan is a disaster for small businesses and discourages any of the surviving businesses to expand beyond 49 employees. As I discussed in my previous book, this health care bill is socialism on American soil. In a socialist state, businesses are regulated by government much like General Motors in the post-bailout era; many regimes like Hitler's ultimately took control of Austria and other countries by bailouts and absorbing the free market to government control, creeping to a gradual takeover. America does not need a government-regulated system that would decide whether you, I or your grandmother should get a knee replacement, kidney transplant or even pull the plug.

If you think a national health care plan is a good idea, then you must think that other socialist countries who have similar plans are doing a good job. You must be fine with having the breast cancer mortality rate 88 percent higher and the prostate cancer mortality rate 604 percent higher, like it is in the United Kingdom. If you want social-ized health care in the US then you probably know that your wait time will be 200 percent longer, like it is in Canada and the United Kingdom, and you won't have a problem with that. And if you support Obamacare you must be okay with ignoring the fact that most countries with socialized medicine, including Germany, Canada, Australia, New Zealand and the United Kingdom, are dissatisfied with their quality of health care as a population. According to the National Center for Policy Analysis[6], this is the reality of socialized medicine, and this is what Americans are asking for when they support Obamacare.

If you are a fan of socialized health care you are an idiot, because why would you follow something so blindly that has historically taken away freedom choice and delivered worse medical care? The attitude of our generation is that we would rather have something crappy that we receive for free than great care that we have to work for.

The scary thing is the government knows that the ACA is not better for the American people—which the numbers show—and that is why our elected officials have voted for themselves to have an entirely different set of benefits. That is also why the Obama Administration handed out waivers to companies that were buddy-buddy with the administration. The fact that Barack Obama, the man who proposed the bill, won't even use it should be a huge red flag to everyone.

Sure, there are some people out there who genuinely cannot afford health care, and many have access to Medicare, but for the most part people who do not have health care are victims of their own misplaces priorities. How many of those families who do not have health care do you think have two cars, a flat screen television, eat out a few times a week or have a fancy cell phone? A family cell phone bill can run about $250 a month, not to mention the price of the phone. Ironically, that is quite similar to the monthly premium for many health care programs (before Obamacare).

Would you think it was outrageous if everyone had and paid for their own health care, but the government required everyone to buy and use cell phone plans of at least $250 a month?

Below is a comment posted on Facebook by a brilliant, young physician by the name of Dr. Roger Starner Jones and addressed to President Obama. I used it in my previous book but felt that it needed to be reiterated here because it is a great example of how the American people seem to have backwards priorities.

Dear Mr. President:

During my shift in the Emergency Room last night, I had the pleasure of evaluating a patient whose smile revealed an expensive shiny gold tooth, whose body was adorned with a wide assortment of elaborate and costly tattoos, who wore a very expensive brand of tennis shoes and who chatted on a new cellular telephone equipped with a popular R&B ringtone.

While glancing over her patient chart, I happened to notice that her payer status was listed as "Medicaid"! During my examination of her, the patient informed me that she smokes more than one pack of cigarettes every day, eats only at fast-food take-outs, and somehow still has money to buy pretzels and beer. And, you and our Congress expect me to pay for this woman's health care? I contend that our nation's "health care crisis" is not the result of a shortage of quality hospitals, doctors or nurses. Rather, it is the result of a "crisis of culture" a culture in which it is perfectly acceptable to spend money on luxuries and vices while refusing to take care of one's self or, heaven forbid, purchase health insurance. It is a culture based in the irresponsible credo that "I can do whatever I want to because someone else will always take care of me". Once you fix this "culture crisis" that rewards irresponsibility and dependency, you'll be amazed at how quickly our nation's health care difficulties will disappear.

Respectfully,
ROGER STARNER JONES, MD

The solution is simple and, as usual, involves less government interference. First, repeal all of it, people will not die Nancy Pelosi, health care existed before Barrack Obama. It will be almost like it never happened and we will just chalk it up to one of the worst ideas ever. Then the government can pass a bill that gives all health care companies and their customers the ability to compete across state lines for consumers like Donald Trump is trying to do now. Those companies who choose not to—take note of the ability to choose given back to the private sector—would be losing valuable clients.

That's a great plan, huh? In one paragraph we were able to nail down a better plan than Obama's 2,000 pages that no one actually read before voting on, but that is another issue.

As for pre-existing conditions, this is one topic where I could see an argument for the need of government intervention. As capitalists know, and we all should accept, it's not evil for a company to want to be profitable. A company's goal is to make money, and when they do, as we saw with President Trump's tax cuts, they give it back to their employees and reinvest in their businesses. This is why insurance companies tend to turn away patients with preexisting conditions because it is not a good investment for the company. Where the government could really help is not by mandating these companies to essentially commit to losing money on a client, but rather assist these individuals with their increased premiums. This would cost fractions of the proposed blanket coverage for everyone and still give the government an avenue to spend our money as we know they love to do.

Another huge issue that is actually costing states and local medical facilities is the increasing number of malpractice suits. Some states have doctors fleeing due to the legal scrutiny just to make simple prescriptions. As a country we need to rationalize this, and it's a fine line between regulation and personal responsibility. Many out there who we might call ambulance chasers are eager to make a buck and this needs to be put in check. So, raise the stakes on the plaintiff. If they lose the suit against the medical facility or doctor, then they should have to pay for their lawyer as well as the defendant's lawyer fees and maybe even a fee for damages to the hospital. That would make us think twice about suing for a Band-Aid put on wrong.

The bottom line here is that health care today is not a right, nor should it be. My generation needs a lesson on what are rights and what are privileges. The ability to choose is a right that Americans have, and when the government falsely categorizes a privilege like health care as a right they take away what is an actual right.

CHAPTER SEVEN
REFORM THE AMERICAN
TAX SYSTEM

BRINGING EQUALITY BACK TO THE
AMERICAN TAX STRUCTURE

"It is a paradoxical truth that tax rates are too high today and tax revenues are too low - and the soundest way to raise revenues in the long run is to cut rates now."

JOHN F. KENNEDY

"I will cut taxes - cut taxes - for 95 percent of all working families, because, in an economy like this, the last thing we should do is raise taxes on the middle class."

BARACK OBAMA

"250 years ago we fought the revolutionary war over a 2 percent tax hike in a breakfast beverage, continue to tax us and there will be another revolution."

CARL HIGBIE

AND THEN THERE was the Trump tax cuts that the left said would literally kill people... reality. Despite what CNN says, people got bigger paychecks, the economy boomed, business moved companies and assets back to America and so on and so forth... But I digress.

Prior to these massive and long overdue cuts, the way our tax system was set up the average American was basically working for free for four to five months out of the year. This is because the government steals an unnecessarily large portion of Americans' income only to waste over 50 percent of the collected amount. In our past and very complicated tax code, the harder you worked and the more money you made, the more you were penalized in the form of tax brackets.

Before Reagan's tax cuts, the top 1 percent paid 18 percent of all federal income tax, with the highest tax bracket paying a 70 percent rate. When Reagan reduced the highest tax bracket to a 28 percent rate, the tax revenue generated by the same top 1 percent of wage earners doubled, and their total contribution rose to 36 percent of the total federal income tax revenue.[1] This is possible because when people have more money in their paycheck, they invest in the economy through purchasing goods or starting businesses, creating more wealth in the economy that equals more dollars that are eligible to tax, just like we saw with President Trump. Weird, it's almost like basic economics and history are not taught to 50 percent of the country.

This is proof that lowering taxes does benefit the rich and their

companies, but it also benefits the middle class and the poor because with corporate expansion comes more jobs for the middle class. Any idiot knows that, and if you are going to be penalized for exceptionalism then less people are going to strive for it. This is dictating American's satisfaction with mediocrity along with our useless participation trophies.

In 2014 the top 1 percent of tax payers, about 3 million people, paid for 45.7 percent of the total income taxes according to an estimation by the Tax Policy Center.[2] The top 20 percent of taxpayers paid for 83.9 percent of the total income taxes in this country. The bottom 40 percent paid for 0 percent of the total income taxes, and somehow some even managed to earn money from it. These facts are all easily accessible, but people still think the upper-class does not pay enough. President Obama summed up the left's view well when he said, "I do think that at a certain point you have made enough money."

It's pretty ironic that Congress thinks it's fair that they get to decide how much money you are allowed to make, but you don't get to decide how much money they are allowed to make.

Wake up, America. The same people who keep Americans employed and, for the most part, keep our country funded are being demonized by the left for not paying their fair share. And the same ones who are whining about successful people because they want them to pay even more in taxes hoard their own money and assets. As a result of President Trump's tax cuts, you have Nancy Pelosi so out of touch that she says that $1,000 bonuses being awarded all across the country are crumbs. How out of touch is that? I realize that to her and her ivory tower ilk that is what they spend on a hair stylist, but to normal people that is a mortgage payment or down payment to replace a fifteen-year-old car.

It is pretty funny that all of these Democrats who propose tax hikes, especially for the rich, almost never donate to support their own ideology, even when they are the rich ones. It is a fact that the taxes you pay are the minimum you are required by the IRS. Anyone at any time has the opportunity to pay more.

In Virginia, Democrats even had the chance to live up to their own policies, and they proved themselves to be the hypocrites we thought they were. In 2002 Virginia, among other states, started a fund called the "Tax Me More Fund" as a way for advocates of higher taxes to put their money where their mouth is. In an eight-year period, it only collected $12,887.04, with 2006 only bringing in $19.36.[3] This is very pathetic considering that Tim Kaine, Hillary Clinton's vice presidential candidate, former Senator and the Governor of Virginia from 2006 to 2010, personally proposed about $6 billion in tax increases during his term. Proposing those kinds of increases and considering his own large salary, you would think that Mr. Kaine would have donated to the fund himself, but I could find no record of that.

So liberals, before you go and steal more of my money, because that is what a tax increase would be at this point, stop being hypocrites and live by your own ideals. I do not work hard so our officials can have more power, and the rest of America shouldn't stand for it either.

The more money we are forced to pay in taxes, the less motivated people are to excel and the more motivated they are to find loopholes around those taxes. Taxes become suppressive and demotivate American exceptionalism. Our leaders have used class warfare to drum up public support for higher taxes on the rich solely because it gets them votes. When these successful entrepreneurial CEOs pass costs off to the consumers or lay off employees to combat the raised costs of operation, the same stupid governments officials that should be held responsible shrug their shoulders and blame it on the rich for being greedy. Then the middle class is pit against the job creators during their next campaign, essentially running on crushing the economy and job market and disguising it as getting the rich to pay their fair share.

Outrageous? Yes, but this happens because we the people sometimes vote morons like this into office. They make outrageous proposals, like the $15 to $20 per hour minimum wage, that are counterproductive to economic success but sound great to the masses. In Connecticut when the minimum wage was raised to $10.10 an hour, a number of fast food restaurants laid off employees. They were replaced by computers because at the new rate it became more economical to invest in technology over unskilled workers. This resulted in more people not having a job, furthering the already abysmal Connecticut job numbers. This is the reality of many of the left's policies.

Anyone with the slightest amount of education should understand that we as a society need to pay taxes to maintain a functioning country, but there needs to be more accountability for our officials who dictate the tax code. There is a happy medium, but despite what Michael Moore thinks, more taxes are certainly not the answer.

"America is not broke! Not by a long shot! The country is awash in wealth and cash. It's just that it's not in your hands! It has been transferred in the greatest heist in history, from the workers and consumers, to the banks and portfolios of the uber-rich," Moore said in a speech in 2011.[4]

Well... Here come the pesky little facts, Mr. Moore. That same year Walter E. Williams, economist and frequent contributor to Townhall.com, considered how long we would be able to sustain the government if we taxed the richest in the country 100 percent.[5] He found that if the government took all of the earnings that year of those who made above $250,000 a year, we would only be able to fund the government for less than five months. To try to finish out the year the government could go after all of the Fortune 500 companies' profits and the stocks, and next the billionaire's businesses and airplanes, but even then, the government would be short a couple of months, according to Mr. William's calculations.

And after 2011, how do we pay for 2012? The budget that year was even larger. We already took all the billionaires' and the Fortune 500's money, therefore they have nothing to invest in new growth. Who do you tax now? Whoever is in office can blame whoever they want, but the fact of the matter is that capitalism would be dead, and Americans' lives would be in shambles.

The rich do not pile their money up and sleep on it like the politicians want their progressive constituents to believe. They put it into the economy, investing it into growth and venture capital. If you believe the left's narrative that the rich are greedy, then it would be easy to understand that they always want to make more money. They do this by investing in things that grow, like companies, which oddly need to hire employees and in effect create jobs. This is how they got rich in the first place.

Even Michael Moore, the one who thinks capitalism is a scheme, does this, only instead of on Wall Street he does this in the movie industry. America needs to start calling out the celebrities and congressmen who accuse the rich of not doing enough for the hypocrites they are, and more importantly, to stop embracing idiots who don't understand the very system they are denouncing.

A simple fix to our tax problems would be a flat tax on income. Our system is so complicated that you may end up paying more or less every year depending on who does your taxes. I propose a 10 percent federal tax on all money earned. Wealthy, middle class or poor, we would all pay the same rate. Second, I propose a maximum deduction of $50,000 a year. When it comes to social issues, the left always cries out that everyone is created equal and should be treated equal. If you want equal rights and equal opportunity for everyone, you might as well tax us all equally too, because you wouldn't want to be a hypocrite, would you? Our generation has been so clearly brainwashed by the left that they seriously think it is fair to force the rich to pay a higher percentage of their wealth than everyone else.

With a flat tax rate of 10 percent, if you make a million dollars,

$100,000 would be paid to the government; if you made $50,000 then you would pay $5,000 to the government, both less your deductions. States would be entitled to impose their own taxes, but federal taxes would be simple. There would be no deductions outside of charity, child credits, mortgage interest and a handful of others. This would motivate the greedy rich people to spread wealth by those who have earned its terms, and not those of some inexperienced bureaucrat who has never held a private sector job.

I'm sure liberals would even be shocked to learn that our country was able to survive without a federal income tax once, and the 1913 amendment that started it was the Republicans' doing. Unlike how it sounds, the Republicans really didn't propose an income tax because they felt the government wasn't taking enough money from people, but they did so to try to stop the Democrats who did want an income tax. As you can see, this backfired badly for the Republicans and US citizens.

Income taxes were used temporarily by the federal government to help pay for the Civil War[6], according to an article in *Business Insider* by Christina Sterbenz. In 1865 the Supreme Court ruled that a permanent income tax would be unconstitutional, but of course the left, who must have always had little respect for the Constitution, tried to sneak it into a tariff bill. Knowing they would need a majority of states to sign off an amendment allowing the federal government to collect an income tax, and thinking that this would be nearly impossible, the Republics proposed an amendment as a message to Democrats to stop their efforts. The Sixteenth Amendment was, indeed, approved and the income tax added to the US Constitution.

But our country isn't struggling because the Republicans failed in their attempts to stop the taxing of Americans. It is struggling because so many administrations have felt that the government could do a better job of redistributing of American's wealth than the individuals or businesses that earned that wealth. Never in the history of the world has any government been able to legislate people into prosperity. And this situation can be solved without government intervention. In fact, undoing the government's backwards economics would speak volumes for progress; an example is the growth during President Trump's first year.

The crushing regulations, laws and taxes imposed on small businesses also need to be addressed. What is currently proposed is a penny here and a dollar there, but it all adds up. America's small businesses produce approximately two thirds of all the new private sector jobs in this country[7], but cannot solely support the system individually. On the other hand, the large-scale failure of small businesses can single handedly collapse our economy. The all-knowing Democrats need to understand that often small businesses struggle to make payroll, pay fees and maintain operating costs, especially when the toughest season financially for businesses is winter, and tax season falls right after. If the government were to tax small businesses more, many businesses that are already suffering would fail. If presidents like Barack Obama had *any* real-world business experience personally or in their cabinet, they would know this.

If the big companies are taxed into failure, then the little companies who support the needs of corporations, or who are hired as contractors of the big companies, will die too. The fact that I am not a millionaire, a big company CEO or a presidential advisor—I do not even have a college degree—should say that this is not a difficult concept to comprehend. Small businesses are trying desperately to keep their heads above water, but all the government does is hold them down. Sooner or later they will drown.

With our country's businesses struggling, one of the first tasks our generation should tackle is getting rid of the corporate tax. Before you have a mental breakdown at the thought of completely doing away with a tax, consider how many businesses would thrive if the corporate tax was eliminated. When we cut it down to the low twenties, look at the hundreds of billions of dollars that came pouring back in. Even more, how many other countries would move their businesses here? Other countries would invest and spend money in the US that would be taxed revenue, a tax that could be based on their contribution to the world economy and the American economy. In the same light, there would be no tax cuts for American companies who outsource their jobs.

In the end, it's always the America people who will lose the more we are taxed. President Reagan was right when he said, "Only people pay taxes, all the taxes. Government just uses business as a kind of sneaky way to help collect taxes." Stealing Americans' money does not create wealth; Americans create wealth themselves. It's an easy solution: force our government to get out of our wallets.

CHAPTER EIGHT
REDUCE THE FEDERAL GOVERNMENT

TIME TO TAKE A CHAINSAW TO GOVERNMENT BUREAUCRACIES

"If you have ten thousand regulations you destroy all respect for the law."

WINSTON CHURCHILL

"I have little interest in streamlining government or in making it more efficient...my aim is not to pass laws, but to repeal them."

BARRY GOLDWATER

THE FEDERAL GOVERNMENT took in about $3.5 trillion dollars in 2016 but it a proposed budget of about $3.9 trillion. Somehow that doesn't seem to add up.

In 2016 our government spent about a half a billion dollars more than it had. Officials did this because they didn't have to deal with the consequences. Instead, the results of overspending year after year will fall on the backs of my generation. It blows my mind that, in a time when protests and riots over social issues are so prevalent, more people are not rioting over the fact that the government is taking them to the cleaners.

We can start by transforming our culture and reforming the tax code, but really chipping away at our debt will require large cuts to federal spending. Although Ronald Reagan joked during his presidency that "the nearest thing to eternal life we will ever see on this earth is a government program," it is time for us to prove him wrong; that is why we elected Donald Trump. Eliminating the Departments of Education, Energy, Commerce, Labor, Housing and Urban Development and the Environmental Protection Agency would help drastically. This would cut hundreds of thousands of needless government jobs and save billions of dollars for the taxpayers.

Now before you lose your mind like the few readers on the left are, of course people are going to be outraged by the loss of government jobs and programs, but... get over it. Those jobs are essentially unproductive deadweights; I know this because I was a senior appointee that oversaw program on top of useless program that were created solely to give people jobs and promotions without achieving any discernable function. They produce nothing and cost the taxpayers billions a year. If many of these employees enter the private sector, they may actually contribute to our economy and provide needed services and skills rather than leeching taxpayer dollars. All of this, combined with the deregulation of the private sector, would allow them to transition into real jobs that would be and have been created.

Grab an ax—and liberals grab a box of tissues and get ready for a good cry—because I'm about to talk about cutting government jobs and departments.

THE DEPARTMENT OF EDUCATION

How the federal government has gotten away with having so much control over education when that function is not in the Constitution is mind blowing. The current Department of Education (ED) is relatively new, created in 1980, has a budget of approximately $68 billion and employs 4,400 people.[1]

According to ED, this department is important because it handles financial aid for education, highlights national issues on education, though it has never highlighted itself as an issue funny enough, stops discrimination in schools and collects data on students and schools.

Though the existing department is new, the idea of it is not. It started in 1867 to collect data on schools to help states create better educational systems. What happened then, like most government departments, is a snowball effect. As the years went by the department grew bigger with more responsibilities, and by responsibilities I mean more useless, redundant tasks and, of course, more costs to taxpayers. Over the years the name of the agency might have changed, probably to try to confuse tax payers, but the idea is still the same. The federal government uses this department and billions of taxpayers' dollars to collect unneeded data on students.

Most liberals have probably never actually read the Constitution, so it might be news to them that the issue of education is not mentioned in it. This *should* make the issue of education fall under the jurisdiction of the Tenth Amendment and, therefore, under jurisdiction of the states, but somehow the federal government has gotten away with taking control of it. The founding fathers expected education to be handled by state and local governments because those closest to the schools would best know those students' needs related to their region and demographic.

The Department of Education acknowledges that they play a small part in the country's education, yet they have no problem taking more and more taxpayers' money. Of the total amount spent nationally on education, only 10.8 percent of it is contributed by the federal government, yet they seem to be involved in more than 10 percent of the decisions and forced regulations on schools.

Does anyone really think that if this department was cut there would be no way students could find financial aid to go to school, national issues on education would never be known, students would be facing more discrimination, or our schools would fail because the federal government didn't collect any data? No, somehow Americans would still be educated, and they would probably be even better educated. Parents, communities and teachers know what's best for students and they are capable of deciding what that is without any federal government help. If this department was cut we would be saving a large chunk of money and children's education would be back in the hands of the parents.

THE DEPARTMENT OF ENERGY

The Department of Energy (DOE) is not only a waste of taxpayers' hard-earned money, it is harmful to our country. According to their website their mission "is to ensure America's security and prosperity by addressing its energy, environmental and nuclear challenges through transformative science and technology solutions."[2]

Whenever the government tells you that they are going to create anything of value while creating another department, it is a lie. The free market creates, and the government hinders by enforcing harmful regulations and restrictions; some, through very few, are in fact needed while most are burdensome. With the rare exception of the Manhattan Project and a handful of other immediate need-based projects, the government does not have a great track record of creating innovative technology. Private sector innovation will always outpace government regulation and subsidization. So, if the free market is what creates solutions to energy and environmental problems, and these problems are often even created by the government itself, why would we need a department to do so? Cut it!

The DOE was created in 1977 and combined already existing programs for energy regulation, analysis and the government's nuclear project. Until this time, with the exception of the nuclear field, these tasks were the private sector's responsibility. According to the DOE, "Americans expected private industry to establish production, distribution, marketing, and pricing policies. When free market conditions were absent, Federal regulations were established to control energy pricing."

But free market conditions are never just absent. The government enforces more regulations, which makes the free market less effective, and then the government blames the free market for the problems that they created in order to convince the public that more regulations are needed to fix the problem. Somehow the country didn't crash and burn before the 1970s when the DOE was established, and yet today the government has convinced the public that almost $30 billion needs to be given to the department for the betterment of the country. Ironically at the time of publication, this department is run by the man that stood on stage in 2012 as a presidential candidate the promised to cut it entirely, Rick Perry. Unreal!

The DOE promises in its mission to protect the future of Americans through science and technology, but you rarely hear of new technologies created by the DOE. Great technologies like fracking, which is the process of drilling into the earth to extract oil and natural gas and could make the US energy independent, was not created by the department. The DOE receives billions of dollars to tackle energy issues like this and come up with better solutions, and yet with no government money the private sector was able to do it first.

But the DOE does have a small useful job, and that is its work on nuclear waste and weapons. These weapons are important for the national security of our country, but also require maximum security.

Like I said before, the best and most innovative technology is rarely created by a government department. The US military secures the worlds' most dangerous weapons, including nukes, and often works hand-in hand-with the DOE. I know this because I was directly involved as a SEAL. How about letting the military takeover that small percent of responsibility the DOE covers and dump the whole department?

When they aren't crushing innovation and working with nuclear weapons, the DOE tackles important issues. In 2015 they warned people that pumpkins are causing climate change.[3] The department broadcasted this important news on their website, and informed people that most of the pumpkins produced in the US end up in the garbage and eventually decompose into a greenhouse gas which is harmful to the environment. This was probably approved by the same idiot that sent over half a million taxpayer dollars to study a shrimp running on a treadmill.

These are the kind of energy issues that the DOE is spending billions of dollars to address, and somehow Democrats can't seem to find anything in the budget that needs to be cut. The government has duped the public into thinking they are capable of creating useful technology and tackling environmental issues, and they have done so by robbing the taxpayers of billions of dollars. They are stealing our money and using it to give themselves more power so that they can steal more of our money. Cut the department and put the sole responsibility of creating new energy into the hands of the free market where it belongs.

THE DEPARTMENT OF LABOR

The Department of Labor (DOL) now spends over $13 billion and has about 18,000 full-time equivalent employees. This department has been around for about 100 years, and according to their mission statement their job is "to foster, promote, and develop the welfare of the wage earners, job seekers, and retirees of the United States; improve working conditions; advance opportunities for profitable employment; and assure work-related benefits and rights."[4] Now to be fair, while in Washington, I worked with the DOL, but I saw their biggest value as making the connection between job creators and potential employees. Guess what private sector entity nailed that one already? Social media platforms like Monster.com and LinkedIn.

The DOL is responsible for meddling in private business. One of their accomplishments includes setting the federal minimum wage to $7.25 an hour in 2009. If you have ever had a hard time finding an entry-level job or being overworked in your entry-level job because your employer couldn't afford to hire another employee, you can thank the DOL. Somehow we have allowed a group of people in Washington, DC to think that they know better how to run a business than small-business owners and CEOs. Again, I have worked with many people there, most are great folks, but almost all are government bureaucrats that don't understand business beyond a PowerPoint presentation.

They also brag about protecting the safety of employees and fighting for better wages and benefits, but like every other useless department, all of this could be done by the free market. If you don't want to work at a place that pays you badly and puts you in danger, then you can find a different job. And if that employer wants to keep you they will be forced to compete with the wages and benefits of other employers.

America, if you are paying for something and you have to ask yourself how it benefits you, then it is probably not needed. The DOL does not improve wages and welfare of Americans, choices do. As usual when the government gets out of the way and allows the free market to thrive, more jobs will become available through supply and demand. The result of this is workers having more choices, which forces employers to compete for employees, thus creating a higher-wage environment. This is something that is a tried and true economic reality, but the DOL is not and is a waste of money.

DEPARTMENT OF COMMERCE

The Department of Commerce irks my soul because its very existence suggests that some people, somewhere in Washington, DC, believe that the government can regulate and foster commerce better than the market itself, never mind the apparent redundancy with the Department of Labor. This department was created in 1903 and according to its website, "the Secretary of Commerce serves as the voice of US business within the President's Cabinet. The Department works with businesses, universities, communities, and the Nation's workers to promote job creation, economic growth, sustainable development, and improved standards of living for Americans."[5] This leads me to ask, then, what the does the DOL do?

Commerce sucks about $10 billion from our budget each year and employs around 47,000 bureaucrats. I have never benefited from anything that they have done, but according to their website they help drive business... Right.

If the government ever takes credit for helping successful businesses be successful, or to know anything about how a business actually works, it is lying. Would a business owner take advice from an organization that is terribly in debt because year after year they spend more than they have? That wouldn't make any sense, so why does it make sense for businesses to listen to a government agency that does that?

The last time I checked, not one of those agencies invented any new product or created a real job. And why would we expect that? We receive almost all good things and life-improving innovations from the free market, not the government. But once again, a bureaucratic monster slows our economic growth and hinders our generation as we try to restore America. Like every other department that should be cut, the solution is to not do anything but to sit back and watch the free market work its magic. The shocking irony of all this is that every politician ridiculed Donald Trump about his promises to bring jobs back. He cited his business experience and was laughed at, but now our economy is booming. Barrack Obama even said, "Do you have a magic wand?" This displayed the clear lack of understanding of career government officials on the job market... Abracadabra!

THE DEPARTMENT OF HOUSING AND URBAN DEVELOPMENT

I have a dear friend at the top of Department of Housing and Urban Development's command structure who is genuinely working hard on this front, but nevertheless, I must state my analysis. To me, HUD is perplexing. Why would a program for housing and urban development exist anywhere outside Soviet Russia?

This department was part of President Johnson's Great Society program, which in itself should be a reason to cut it, and was intended to help develop housing policies, especially for inner cities. If you have listened to any history on President Johnson you would know the creation of this agency was about votes, not actual people or housing. HUD's mission "is to create strong, sustainable, inclusive communities and quality affordable homes for all. HUD is working to strengthen the housing market to bolster the economy and protect consumers; meet the need for quality affordable rental homes; utilize housing as a platform for improving quality of life; build inclusive and sustainable communities free from discrimination, and transform the way HUD does business."[6] To deliver on this lofty goal the department requested almost $50 billion for 2016.

Like most other federal government departments, there is no constitutional argument for keeping this department because it is not the government's job to house people. It sounds like a nice idea, and maybe in the short term it is, but in the long term no good can come from a government handout. And again, if the government tells you they are going to strengthen the market that is a lie.

HUD has also been surrounded by scandal. In previous administrations, those at the top of the department have been caught abusing their power to do favors for others for political gain. This was even a problem during the Reagan administration, which proves it doesn't matter who is in charge because power corrupts. These problems are not just isolated incidents, and the fact that a department that has proven itself to be corrupt multiple times is still receiving billions of dollars from taxpayers is despicable.

The free market can dictate urban development and housing practices; however, if the free market was not forced to provide risky home loans, our current economic standing may have been much better. Employing that many bureaucrats and spending that much money, when billions of dollars are already being spent to help those less fortunate with housing, is unjustifiable. So, if you haven't guessed a theme, the best solution to housing is to allow the free market to do its job and to eliminate HUD.

THE ENVIRONMENTAL PROTECTION AGENCY

The department of redundancy department, or The Environmental Protection Agency (EPA) has been riddled with scandal under every administration, even under President Trump. It may not even be a true cabinet department, but the agency is viewed with the same gravitas as a department, so we will treat it as such.

Not shockingly, it mirrors a litany of other state and federal agencies and claims to be responsible for assessing the environment, researching environmental issues and educating the public about possible environmental concerns.[7] Ironically, they were also responsible for the worst chemical contamination incident of 2015 when they dumped tons of waste into Cement Creek and the Animas River in Colorado.[8] But please lecture us on the environment.

The EPA's powers are somewhat vast, having the ability to make its own regulations beyond Congress and possessing its own enforcement measures, such as heavy fines and oppressive sanctions. Is this unconstitutional? Citizens can seek relief only from the US federal courts, although they must do so through the representation of pricey environmental lawyers if they wish to stand a chance.

Proposed by Richard Nixon, the EPA was intended to streamline environmental protection by having Congress delegate its power. This agency completely erodes the founder's intention to create checks and balances in the government and, as a result, it has ballooned into a gigantic government monster. In 2015 the EPA spent more than $8 billion and employed more than 15,000 people.

The agency claims to protect the public, but what it really does is slow economic growth. The PolyMet Mining Corporation knows this well. They have been battling the EPA in Minnesota for more than five years and have already spent more than $22 million to try to build a copper and nickel mine in the northeastern part of the state.[9] These resources that would be mined are used in many everyday objects, and the mine itself could create thousands of jobs and help boost the economy in the state. There is little, if any evidence, that this mine would pollute the water in the area, yet the EPA won't allow them to start building without the official green light. It is absolutely cruel to force Americans to be jobless and suffer economically simply because a government agency thinks it knows better than everyday Americans what is best for them.

The left tries to convince our generation that the government always does what is best for the people and the public only cares about themselves. Newsflash: the people who live by the mine are the ones who have to live with the water, not the EPA bureaucrats, so don't you think that they would care more about the environment around them than distant bureaucrats? If the people in the local area want the mine, the government needs to step out of the way and stop pretending like they always know what's best.

As proof that a government agency can indeed be more pathetic and hypocritical than I originally thought: until 2013 the EPA still had 18.4 million publications of paper records that it was storing at a cost of more than $1.5 million per year, according to an article in Rare.[10] A government agency that is meant to protect the environment has how many dead trees sitting in storage? Why wasn't the same agency that claims to be experts on what is best for Americans and the environment because they have the best technology and scientific information storing its documents digitally like every other modern company and organization? If that isn't a perfect example of how screwed up these government departments are, I don't know what is.

Calling to eliminate the EPA is not a new idea. In the 2012 Republican primary candidates like Rick Perry and Newt Gingrich called for the end of the agency[11], and in the 2016 Republican primary so did Donald Trump, Ted Cruz and Marco Rubio.[12]

At this point, it's just common knowledge that the agency forestalls development, kills jobs and sucks resources from the economy as businesses try to comply with needless and complex regulations.

If this agency is eliminated, will the US environment erode into a polluted mess? Of course not. People want to protect the environment because it's in their best interest, so they will make sure that it stays clean. If a company is polluting the environment and the public doesn't like that, they will stop supporting that company. It's called capitalism and it will do a much better job than the EPA has ever done.

And last but certainly not least...

CNCS (THE CORPORATION NATIONAL AND COMMUNITY SERVICE)

While not a cabinet agency, CNCS has a seat at the table in cabinet affairs. I was fortunate enough to be appointed as the chief of external affairs, which meant I was the face of the agency. This is relatively small agency at about $1.2 billion, but to us normal people that is still a ton of money. Let me preface this section by saying that the intent of this agency is good; however, in keeping with true government fashion it has developed into an entangled bureaucracy that hinders more than it helps. According to the website—a disaster to navigate that I spent the majority of my time there trying to rebuild —the mission is to help "millions of Americans improve the lives of their fellow citizens through service. Working hand in hand with local partners, we tap the ingenuity and can-do spirit of the American people to tackle some of the most pressing challenges facing our nation."[13]

According to public records, CNCS spends half of its $1.2 billion budget, funded by tax payers, for internal operations that I will explain later and then grants the other half to nonprofits across the country through actual cash grants or direct service assistance. Sounds great but think about this for a second: the agency confiscates more than a billion dollars in taxes, spends half to merely exist, and then gives the other half right back to the same people and programs that the government took it from in the first place.

While I was a senior appointee there, I had the chance to travel all over the country to see the programs that we were supporting. Even though these programs knew I represented the agency that funded them, almost every single person I met with took a moment to highlight the dysfunction the saw from their experience in working with CNCS. This was universal and not unique to a few. So why didn't anyone fix it? Enter government programs...

To talk to a program, such as the one dealing with opioid addiction in California, I would follow the prescribed flow chart and first email the Washington, DC-based Office of Field Liaison. This office was upstairs from mine, but it required written notification. The liaison would then email their state counterpart, who would then email the state director, who could then email the actual program. The response would follow the same pattern on the way back and, as you may imagine, this could take weeks, if I ever got an answer at all. If you are like me, you are probably as confused as to why this system exists as I was. Initially I attempted to navigate this process until I found that I could just pick up the phone and call the program directly. This accomplished everything I needed but set off a firestorm with the career bureaucrats, namely the acting Chief Executive Officer and Chief of Staff who valued structure over function in all cases.

For example, thirty days prior to Thanksgiving I asked what any of the thousands of community service programs we oversaw would be doing for Thanksgiving in their communities. What followed was just one reason that this agency was slotted for a zero budget by Mick Mulvaney and the White House. Despite multiple follow ups with all departments, no one could provide me with a SINGLE activity that AmeriCorps or Senior Corps were doing on Thanksgiving! I could not have been more vocal about my concern for this. But here is the kicker: the day after Thanksgiving, I received dozens of Google alerts talking about the programs we were involved with across the country! It's also important to note that prior to me canceling the contract, the agency spent millions of dollars for external public relations support that was supposed to monitor media for this type of thing. The PR agency found no media mentions; my free Google alerts did, however. Also overseeing the PR section of the agency, I never even so much as spoke to the people doing our "PR" despite multiple requests... This is government.

So, knowing that the system was broken, for Christmas I instructed my right-hand hire (Dan Pollack) to reach out to our grantees directly to find out what we were doing and how we could help promote or get involved with their activities. Unbeknownst to him, I simultaneously tasked my deputy (Marc Young) with the same thing. My deputy, with an entire department of 20 people at his disposal, identified one program while my guy who reached directly out to the grantees found dozens. Dan was able to get media support for them through television and print and coordinated support from our local representatives and the state and national offices ultimately making our agency look great. Sounds like congratulations were in order, right? Nope. Here is the conversation I had when returning from the holiday with our acting bureaucrat CEO.

CEO: Carl you can't just pick up the phone and call the grantees directly.

Me: Why?

CEO: Because that is the job of the office of field liaison.

Me: But we tried that for the last holiday and nothing got done, we also tried that route for this holiday and they only turned up one program. The system is broken so I found a way to work around it.

CEO: Well Carl, if you circumvent the appropriate channels, the system doesn't work.

CEO: But the system already doesn't work as evidence of their lack of results, the only way I made it work was by circumventing the system.

CEO: Carl, if you take away their responsibilities they won't have a job to do.

Me: Great, can we shit-can their whole department then?

CEO: No Carl what will that accomplish?

My thoughts were: Aside from saving the tax payers millions of dollars and making us more efficient?

Me: (stunned) This conversation is over. I will continue to do it the way that works.

CEO: (in a chipper tone) OK, great Carl talk soon.

You know that Emoji that is slapping itself in the forehead? That is how I felt. Add this to the fact that our agency granted funds (via service assistance in a VISTA program) to groups like CAIR (Center for American Islamic Relations), and more specifically to the Minnesota chapter whose leader spends much of his time denouncing President Trump. When I tried to make the case that we should remove their grant, our general counsel Tim Noelker, a White House appointee (whose previous law office donated to Hillary Clinton) told me that we could not do that. This was also the guy that didn't lift a finger when I notified him that some of our grants were going to programs that openly served illegal immigrants in defiance of the president. As a presidential appointee it is your job to embody the administration's policies; I didn't see that resolve from Mr. Noelker.

So again, my recommendation: cut it and all the jobs associated with it.

THE BIGGER PICTURE

The government confiscates your money, lights most of it on fire and flushes the ashes down the toilet. There I said it! The government does a horrible job of managing the trillions of dollars it takes from those who earned it.

Our representatives (not leaders) would have you think that without these government departments and agencies, America's children would not be educated, there would be no new innovative energy technologies, employees would be treated terribly, businesses would go under, people would be homeless, and the environment would be ruined. I don't buy it.

Now if you actually believe that, then you deserve to live a life where you are a slave to the government and have no individual liberties. But I can assure you that without all of these departments, without the billions of dollars of hardworking taxpayers' money going down the drain, Americans would be better off.

What all of these departments try to do, but end up just making worse, is something that the free market does on its own. None of these agencies are listed in the Constitution so technically all of these powers are supposed to be solely in the hands of the states. Americans are simply better than this. We don't need help living our lives to the extent the government believes, and we can do it without the government at a fraction of the cost.

PART FOUR

RESTORE NATIONAL
SOVEREIGNTY,
RESTRUCTURE THE
US MILITARY, REIGN
IN THE UN, NATO &
OTHER
INTERNATIONAL
ORGANIZATIONS,
SEEK ENERGY
INDEPENDENCE

CHAPTER NINE
MILITARY

RESTORE AND RESTRUCTURE THE US MILITARY

MAKING OUR MILITARY GREAT...AGAIN

"We're in greater danger today than we were the day after Pearl Harbor. Our military is absolutely incapable of defending this country."

RONALD REAGAN

BEFORE THE JAPANESE attacked Pearl Harbor, America's military totaled less than one and a half million soldiers, sailors, marines, and coastguardsmen. During WWII, Japan's forces totaled more than 6 million, the Germans had 18 million and the Italians had almost 500,000. Compounding matters was the fact that our adversaries' ships outnumbered ours and they had more advanced tanks. Yet America, despite the odds, won. How?

While the answer to that question is complex and best left to military scholars,

I believe a large factor of the victory grew from two things: American exceptionalism and America's citizen-soldier military under the Second Amendment. The men and women who joined the fight understood how to get things done. They were not trained, indoctrinated and forced into the harsh and oftentimes unproductive system that is our current mainstay military. They were farmers, fishermen, mechanics, and men from steel mills and shipyards. In short, they were producers. They brought with them onto the battle fields of Europe and the oceanic theater of the Pacific ingenuity, common sense, and free thought. This was displayed by our success and frequent out-witting of our adversaries. This was all reinforced by the gun culture in America that gave us a leg up to our adversaries, many of which had never touched a gun until they were shipped off to war.

I say this with the utmost respect for our men and women in uniform and the intent is to identify and solve the problem, not solely to criticize. Having served in the military, I can state without hesitation that our military lacks the qualities of the World War II citizen-soldier force. Do not be confused; I believe that our modern military is comprised of good men and women who care for the most part and who want to make a difference in their lives, in the lives of other Americans and for others around the globe. The system now is a mindless and political bureaucracy that thwarts the young service members, and this is leading to a weakened military. The majority of our commanders have become career and rank obsessed, rulers of laws rather than leaders of men.

While in the Navy, I watched as politics sidelined the most productive, sharpest and talented sailors. I observed ambitious and driven men and women leave the military in fear that the unpredictable, inefficient and random promotion system would stall their careers and leave them and their families struggling financially. As I discussed in my first two books, we lived in a system that many of the best who enlisted or sought commissions only served for a few years then moved on to civilian life in pursuit of the meritocracy and a capitalist work force.

Unfortunately, some career soldiers and sailors, like career politicians, turn into bureaucratic zombies as power hungry and self-serving commanders. Many of the few who can withstand the mind-numbing battle rhythm evolve into the rulers-of-laws rather than leaders of men that defeated the axis powers in the forties. These career soldiers and sailors become fixated on their own careers and turn into career-before-country patriots. You don't believe me? Take the mindset, for example, that we lost almost as many troops on the beaches of Normandy in one day as we did in the entire Iraq and Afghanistan wars. Look at how we are fighting: we put the feelings of a nation we invaded before the loss of American lives. We are not willing to do what it takes to win anymore. General James N. Mattis and President Trump have begun to change the course, but it will take time, lots of time.

These military leaders who discourage the free-thinker institute needless rules and protocol that stifle innovation, creativity, and productivity. Or worse yet, they do nothing, keeping their heads down and trying to get by without any conflict. Sadly, they are crushing our military with the weight of their bureaucratic machinery.

I hinted at some of my thoughts on the modern military in my first book, *Battle on the Home Front*, but felt constrained by consequence to fully express the necessary overhaul needed while being an active duty Navy SEAL. I was besieged and barraged by politically motivated officers hell-bent on not making waves so that they could get promoted. My commanders were more concerned with the political fallout of my ideas that could negatively impact their careers than in taking steps to fix a well-known problem themselves. Now that I have left the SEAL teams, I feel fully free to discuss the American military.

I believe that our generation can help strengthen our military by changing the military's promotion system, retirement, service obligations and civilian employee contracts and by instituting new requirements.

Tim Kane says it in the article, "Why Our Best Officers Are Leaving," published in *The Atlantic*. He opens with the most important question, why do talented officers leave the military? He did a survey on US Military Academy graduates to ask what would entice them to leave or stay. The immediate answer was: *The military is creating a command structure that rewards conformism and ignores merit. As a result, it's losing its vaunted ability to cultivate entrepreneurs in uniform.*

And the question was better phrased: *Why does the American military produce the most innovative and entrepreneurial leaders in the country, then waste that talent in a risk-averse bureaucracy?*

Tim Kane focused on a specific example: John Nagl.

Despite being a highly skilled officer who loved the military, John Nagl left before reaching Colonel. A 2010 report from the Strategic Studies Institute of the Army War College reported that "since the late 1980s... prospects for the Officer Corps' future have been darkened by... plummeting company-grade officer retention rates. Significantly, this leakage includes a large share of high-performing officers."

Mr. Kane notes that "the military's problem is a deeply anti-entrepreneurial personnel structure. From officer evaluations to promotions to job assignments, all branches of the military operate more like a government bureaucracy with a unionized workforce than like a cutting-edge meritocracy.... The military has failed to learn the most fundamental lessons of the knowledge economy. And that to hold on to its best officers, to retain future leaders like John Nagl, it will need to undergo some truly radical reforms…".

Of the 250 West Point graduates Mr. Kane interviewed over a fifteen-year period, 93 percent believed that half of "the best officers leave the military early rather than serving a full career… Only 30 percent of the full panel agreed that the military personnel system does a good job promoting the right officers to General, and a mere 7 percent agreed that it does a good job retaining the best leaders."

This is a shockingly bad statistic. If someone's life is on the line, would you not want to retain the best people to make sure they have the best odds in the fight? You don't issue a solider a gun that only shoots straight 30 percent of the time, do you? A private sector company would fail under these conditions. Of those interviewed, 78 percent agreed that it harms national security. And the policy that was instituted to address it was another page out of the most bureaucratic handbook. According to Tim Kane: "Throw money at the problem, in the form of millions of dollars in talent-blind retention bonuses. More often than not, such bonuses go to any officer in the "critical" career fields of the moment, regardless of performance evaluations."

This didn't solve anything because a $30,000 to $90,000 bonus does not retain someone who is competent enough to have the incentive to make double that in the private sector. I have always said that government employees are not supposed to be highly paid for their service; it is the acknowledgement of the merits of the job that are rewarding. In the military neither of these are observed, however.

Kane asked every person he interviewed why he or she left the military and found that 82 percent of respondents were frustrated with military bureaucracy and that 9 out of 10 would have stayed if the military was based on merit.

I could not agree more. While I read this I almost thought I was reading a piece from a more articulate version of myself. I longed for innovation and free thought that would have kept me and many of my colleagues in the military. It was not insubordination to have a different idea; if it was evaluated but not the choice of the commander then so be it. But voicing your idea has become frowned upon. Mr. Kane nailed this down as well, saying "The Pentagon doesn't always reward its innovators. Usually, rebels in uniform suffer at the expense of their ideas. General Mitchell was court-martialed for insubordination in 1925; and who can forget the hostile treatment afforded General Eric Shinseki in 2003 after he testified that 'something on the order of several hundred thousand soldiers' would probably be required to stabilize post-invasion Iraq?

"In a 2007 essay in the Armed Forces Journal, Lieutenant Colonel Paul Yingling offered a compelling explanation for this risk-averse tendency. A veteran of three tours in Iraq, Lieutenant Colonel Yingling articulated a common frustration among the troops: that a failure of generalship was losing the war. His critique focused not on failures of strategy but on the failures of the general-officer corps making the strategy, and of the anti-entrepreneurial career ladder that produced them: 'It is unreasonable to expect that an officer who spends 25 years conforming to institutional expectations will emerge as an innovator in his late forties.'"

I don't make these comments in a vacuum; many people I served with voiced these opinions in private and when I would challenge them to step up and fix the issues, they appeared beaten down. Countless admirals and generals get out and write books about all the things they need to do to change the system... why not step up and change them when in the military? John Nagl did the same in his book, *Learning to Eat Soup with a Knife*. He talked about the surge in Iraq and the big government machine that should have been more acutely tuned to winning the war rather than winning at PowerPoint. Mr. Kane talked about recruiting and retention:

"Simply put, if the Army hopes to stanch the talent bleed, it needs to embrace an entrepreneurial structure, not just culture. That doesn't mean more officers who invent new weapons, but rather a new web of incentives rewarding creative leadership. The military has reinvented itself in this manner before."

I have personally stood in a line following a deployment to receive a Navy Achievement Medal for leading combat operations in Iraq while the person (not a SEAL) in alphabetical order next to me in the medal ceremony received the SAME MEDAL for ensuring all members of the SEAL platoon I was in were properly outfitted with boots. This is the lack of incentive and mindless leadership that discourages good soldiers.

Mr. Kane has a similar idea that I do about an NFL draft-style market:

"Indeed, an internal job market might be the key to revolutionizing military personnel. In today's military, individuals are given 'orders' to report to a new assignment every two to four years. When an Army unit in Korea rotates out its executive officer, the commander of that unit is assigned a new executive officer. Even if the commander wants to hire Captain Smart, and Captain Smart wants to work in Korea, the decision is out of their hands—and another captain, who would have preferred a job in Europe, might be assigned there instead...Giving officers greater voice in their assignments increases both employment longevity and productivity."

It seems like a no brainer but getting a government agency to change anything substantial is nearly apocalyptic.

I included portions of Tim Kane's article because I cannot believe how accurate it is. During my military days, our political discussions frequently ventured into the possibility of incorporating free-market and meritocracy principles into the Navy. Tim Kane discusses many of the concepts and ideas that I and my fellow service members thought the military lacked. I have and still do suggest changing the following areas of the military: the promotion system, retirement, service obligation, civilian employee retention system and education requirements for officers.

PROMOTION SYSTEM

In a word, the military's promotion system is blind. Understandably, the most talented frequently leave the service. This is because they can achieve more in less time in the civilian world and they believe that they will receive more financial rewards for their efforts in the free market with less restrictions to promotions.

In the military and most government jobs, one must be "in zone" for promotion, meaning that the individual has enough time at the current rank level to be eligible for promotion. Simply put, time is key, not effort or talent. In the free market if a job is open then someone will apply, and presumably the best man or woman for the job is hired and the workplace is all the better for it. The free market cares little for artificial concepts, such as "zones" or "time in rank." Qualifications, past performance, and ability reign supreme.

So why not incorporate the free market principles of hiring to the military? Abolish zones, deemphasize time in rank and have open applications for all positions sequentially.[1] The military only stands to gain. If a young Navy lieutenant (pay grade O-3) is incredibly talented, then perhaps he or she could move from division officer to department head position, a position that typically is designated for a lieutenant commander (pay grade O-4) or the next rank above their position. A free market promotion system would help retain the most talented and accelerate them to positions of influence over the career focused individuals. Raw talent would prevail over an artificial career flow chart and the lowest and mediocre evaluated personal would be phased out rather than retained as they are now.

The benefit to such a plan would encourage mediocre officers and enlisted to leave the military or at least designate them to positions of lower authority and influence. This may sound harsh, but the military is in the business of war which is a life and death game and we want our most talented men and women in charge of the military, not the sorry soul who has been around the longest and kissed the right asses.

Additionally, there must be a more stringent process on choosing command leadership as well. Case in point: in 2009 I had a platoon officer-in-charge, or OIC who we will call LT, which is short for lieutenant. His immediate superior was our troop commander, a lieutenant commander or LCDR. The LCDR lacked combat experience, was narcissistic with a massive ego, and had been fired, relieved or failed at three previous positions throughout his career, but he was somehow still in charge. He continued because in the bogus write-ups his true colors were never illustrated. No one above him wanted to ruin his career, and they retained him for the sake of numbers. On the other hand, LT was a very intelligent, hardworking and combat-experienced officer who prioritized the mission first and then the well-being of his men, putting his personal career interests at the bottom of the list. As you may imagine, when you have two men, one who cares more about the mission and the men, and the other who cares more about his personal career path, there were very clear differences that sometimes lead to public conflict.

LT was seen as a threat to LCDR's career if he were to progress and was constantly degraded in his bi-annual evaluations and other matters by LCDR solely because he did not want to conform to the risk-averse and self-serving measures thought to be the norm for LCDR. Upon leaving the command, LT's last evaluation written by LCDR stated "Lacks maturity to lead," essentially ending his professional progression.[2] Every single man under LT strongly disagreed with this evaluation and many even voiced their opposition to our chain of command, including senior enlisted members, but it held no weight and was entered into LT's permanent record. How was someone allowed to write this evaluation who had been fired from the same position the LT held?

Because LT was smart and motivated, the type that should be retained as a SEAL, he decided to give up his career as a SEAL and become a doctor. When a member of the platoon needed medical attention, they hoped LT would be the one to administer it, but ultimately the SEAL teams lost an asset due to poor management. They kept a turd and lost a rock star.

If you are like me, then your jaw is probably on the floor. How does this happen? Well simply put, turds take care of turds and those who speak out against them are outnumbered in the leadership positions and military in general. Now if we had instituted a meritocracy system and a competitive job market in the SEAL teams, this would not have happened, and instead of a deployment of few missions and risking our lives to attempt to win over the hearts and minds of the Iraqi people, we would have been killing bad guys, ultimately reducing the future threat to America that is now ISIS. If commanding officers were to pick their team, much like the NFL drafts, the unworthy officers would be branded as such and not be chosen for positions that help them advance even further. And if you are not picked at all then you would be removed from your occupation, fired just like a real job. Your commanding officer would essentially be the coach, and the rank above him the team owner.

RETIREMENT

In today's military the sorry souls we mentioned often end up riding out their time in the military until retirement. This is because service members can retire with 50 percent of their pay after twenty years; increments rise at twenty-five and thirty years. This includes full benefits and yearly adjustments for inflation. Even the best officers can become complacent, knowing that once they hit twenty years they are all but certain to get a pension and full benefits for life. This must change.

While changing the retirement system may seem drastic or even harsh, one must consider the flaws with our system. For starters, the system encourages service members to become complacent leading up to and after twenty years. Second, the military often uses retirement as tool to manipulate its members. Consider the private sector where individuals usually get a 401(k), oftentimes matched by their employer. This is not true in the military. There is no match for the Thrift Savings Plan. The military puts all its investment into the pension, which does not vest for twenty years and only does so with a certain type of discharge.

This system robs the service member of many financial options and all but enslaves his or her retirement system to the bureaucratic machine. It is used as a wicked tool of control in the military. Too often during legal proceedings did my friends who were legal officers (JAGs) see commands use retirement benefits to force individuals into compromising situations and rulings that sometimes had long-term effects on their lives. Worse, many of these JAGs often had clients who had served in excess of seventeen, eighteen, even nineteen years, and sometimes had only a year or two to until retirement. Sometimes the Navy would swoop in and separate the sailors for minor infractions, thus causing them to lose their retirements.

In the most extreme case I was told about, a service member faced civilian charges outside of military duty. He had put in twenty-four years of service and just wanted to retire to face the charges in Texas and move on with his life. The Navy, prior to any civilian hearing, prosecuted the sailor in the military court and took his retirement at the court-martial, leaving the individual to still face civilian trial anyway. This is double jeopardy and was all done to rob this sailor and his family from his retirement.

Why did the military need to do that? This is also seen in the more recent downsizing of the military known as perform-to-serve or PTS. In the Navy especially, there can only be so many people of each rank in specific jobs or rates. This makes it impossible to advance if your chosen job has its quota in each rank, regardless of your merit. What the military is doing now is pushing service members out by saying they are not performing well enough to meet the requirements of the Navy. In some cases, by no fault of their own, service members are missing their long-awaited retirement by less than a few years. Enough is enough.

We should insist that the military abandon the pension system and use a private sector solution, a matched or fully funded 401(k). With this system the military could, from day one, contribute to a 401(k), the service member could also contribute, and when he or she left the service then they could take the 401(k) along. Service members would no longer serve to get to twenty but rather serve out of patriotism and love for the job. It would also take away from the command's threat of pulling one's retirement, which can be done without any judicial hearings and sometimes at the will of non-legal proceedings by members of a command who are oftentimes legally unqualified to make such a decision. No longer would service members do their time and coast through, appeasing those above them no matter the ridiculousness just to get their retirement.

This problem has not just occurred in a couple of isolated incidents. This was openly expressed by Army Colonel Lawrence on a Facebook post that went viral only to cause the demise of his career from this post.

> *"KABUL, Afghanistan — Throughout my career I have been known to walk that fine line between good taste and unemployment. I see no reason to change that now.*

> *Consider the following therapeutic.*

I have been assigned as a staff officer to a headquarters in Afghanistan for about two months. During that time, I have not done anything productive. Fortunately, little of substance is really done here, but that is a task we do well.

We are part of the operational arm of the International Security Assistance Force commanded by Army Gen. David Petraeus. It is composed of military representatives from all the NATO countries, several of which I cannot pronounce.

Officially, International Joint Command was founded in late 2009 to coordinate operations among all the regional commands in Afghanistan. More likely it was founded to provide some general a three-star command. Starting with a small group of dedicated and intelligent officers, IJC has successfully grown into a stove-piped and bloated organization, top-heavy in rank. Around here, you can't swing a dead cat without hitting a colonel.

For headquarters staff, war consists largely of the endless tinkering with PowerPoint slides to conform with the idiosyncrasies of cognitively challenged generals in order to spoon-feed them information. Even one tiny flaw in a slide can halt a general's thought processes as abruptly as a computer system's blue screen of death.

The ability to brief well is, therefore, a critical skill. It is important to note that skill in briefing resides in how you say it. It doesn't matter so much what you say or even if you are speaking Klingon.

Random motion, ad hoc processes and an in-depth knowledge of Army minutia and acronyms are also key characteristics of a successful staff officer. Harried movement together with furrowed brows and appropriate expressions of concern a la Clint Eastwood will please the generals. Progress in the war is optional.

Each day is guided by the "battle rhythm," which is a series of PowerPoint briefings and meetings with PowerPoint presentations. It doesn't matter how inane or useless the briefing or meeting might be. Once it is part of the battle rhythm, it has the persistence of carbon 14.

And you can't skip these events because they take roll — just like gym class.
The start and culmination of each day is the commander's update assessment. Please ignore the fact that "update assessment" is redundant. Simply saying commander's update doesn't provide the possibility of creating a three-letter acronym. It also doesn't matter that the commander never attends the CUA.
The CUA consists of a series of PowerPoint slides describing the events of the previous 12 hours. Briefers explain each slide by reading from a written statement in a tone not unlike that of a congressman caught in a tryst with an escort. The CUA slides only change when a new commander arrives or the war ends.

The commander's immediate subordinates, usually one- and two-star generals, listen to the CUA in a semi-comatose state. Each briefer has about one or two minutes to impart either information or misinformation. Usually they don't do either. Fortunately, none of the information provided makes an indelible impact on any of the generals.

One important task of the IJC is to share information to the ISAF commander, his staff and to all the regional commands. This information is delivered as PowerPoint slides in e-mail at the flow rate of a fire hose. Standard operating procedure is to send everything that you have. Volume is considered the equivalent of quality.

Next month, IJC will attempt a giant leap for mankind. In a first-of-its-kind effort, IJC will embed a new stovepipe into an already existing stovepipe. The rationale for this bold move resides in the fact that an officer, who is currently without one, needs a staff of 35 people to create a big splash before his promotion board.

Like most military organizations, structure always trumps function.

The ultimate consequences of this reorganization won't be determined until after that officer rotates out of theater.

Nevertheless, the results will be presented by PowerPoint."

See what I'm getting at here?

SERVICE OBLIGATION

Another impediment to our military is that of the service obligation. Most in the military incur a service obligation upon entering the service, completing training or receiving a bonus. Frankly, when service obligations are tied to training or to a bonus, this make perfect sense. However, the many other enlisted personnel must obligate for a term of years without such training or bonuses frequently throughout their careers. This hampers them from wanting to stay in the military due to the potential lost opportunity during their obligation despite their desire. While entirely consensual, this is wrong. I believe that anyone should be allowed to leave the military at any time with few exceptions:

1. During deployments at war, declared by Congress (Yes, Congress, just like Article I of the US Constitution states).
2. Immediately leading up to, or during deployment (once again for engagement declared by Congress).
3. If there is any time left for service obligation due to specialized programs such as BUD/S (SEAL training), flight school, Naval Justice School, and so forth.

These restrictions would create an environment where the military would have to work hard to retain their most talented, and the most talented could easily leave the service to join the private sector. Additionally, tying the restrictions back to a constitutional mandate would force Congress to act according to the constitution when declaring war.

CIVILIAN EMPLOYEE STRUCTURE

Another weight around the military's neck is that of civilian employees. The vast majority of the civilian employees are incredibly nice and devoted people, but in all fairness, for the most part, they do not work nearly as hard as their business-world counterparts and are compensated extremely well with practically lifetime job security. In 2008 non-military federal workers earned an average salary of $67,691 for occupations that exist both in government and the private sector, according to Bureau of Labor Statistics data. The average pay for the same mix of jobs in the private sector was $60,046. I have a personal friend that was a nuclear technician. He spent the minimum required time in service for his job and on a Friday he ended his service as an E-6. The following Monday he began work in the same department in the same room at the same desk that he had worked at for the last five years, only now as a civilian with double the salary, half the workload and almost certain job security. Short of melting down Norfolk, Virginia, he would not lose his job. Therein lies the problem.

There is no guarantee of employment in the business world, nor should there be in the government civilian sector. The difference in pay for essential the same job should also be addressed. The military and the American taxpayer would be far better off having all Department of Defense civilians on a contract system. This way Americans would save more money and the civilian employees would be cheaper and more productive. Additionally, the military could shed the legacy costs of these civilians by avoiding paying for health care and retirement long after these individuals leave Department of Defense employment. It's a small measure, but a measure that would help create a leaner, more cost-effective military.

EDUCATION FOR OFFICERS/ENTREPRENEURIAL DRIVE

One issue that the military suffers from is the lack of entrepreneurial drive and free market experience. The military would be far better off if it were run like a business rather than as a bloated government bureaucracy, which admittedly it is. While our above solutions could help transform the military, so would another simple solution: business education for officers. I proposed that to progress beyond the O-3 level (lower management), officers must have a combat command. Also, in order to be eligible for O-5, an officer would be required to be accepted and successfully complete a one-year internship in a private business. In the internship, the officer's performance evaluations would be written by the business executives.

Simply said, if you can't get accepted or successfully complete an internship, then you are not qualified to make rank. To move to the rank of general or admiral, the officer would again need to get a healthy evaluation from a business leader while serving an additional internship in a management position and show that he or she could lead in both the military and private sector. If the officer failed in the private sector, then retirement would follow, funded by a 401(k), of course.

Too often did I take fire from my superior enlisted service members and officers. I strongly believe that much of the issues were tied to my success in the private sector, where I started my own businesses that had more than a million dollars in gross revenue in its first year and acquired other businesses, all part time. When others in the military discovered this success, I was told I must provide my company's financial information, and when I refused I was threatened with punitive action and received numerous off-the-record counseling sessions. This is the leadership my command should have tried to learn from.

Instead they treated my success as something negative, something to be disdained, feared and mistrusted. On two occasions I was even excused from work to help my superiors render service through my business, only to be reprimanded by them later for my business getting in the way of work. The true fear here is not in the closed-mindedness of those officers, but in their disdain for private industry and the qualities that account for real-world success.

We must break bureaucratic mindlessness. Our great historic military masterminds of the past succeeded based on their life experiences. Most of them were farmers, small business owners and tradesmen first and soldiers second. This taught them to out innovate rather than bark orders and make rules. We can change this with education and experience. Our military must run itself like a business, and we can only get there if our officers think and compete like businessmen.

Generation Y, we are the generation making rank and coming to leadership positions. It is our mandate to adopt, implement and execute successful policies that put a stop to the down fall lest we watch our military's might perish in bureaucracy.

CHAPTER TEN
FOREIGN POLICY

"I am proposing a new foreign policy focused on advancing America's core national interests - so important - promoting regional stability and producing and easing the tensions within our very troubled world."

PRESIDENT DONALD TRUMP

"America is better than everyone else, we should not apologize for it nor try to stoop to other nations, we invented the atom bomb, put a man on the moon and consistently have more gold medals than any other country. Our goal should be to have everyone strive for greatness, not condemn ours."

CARL HIGBIE

"My fear is that the whole island will become so overly populated that it will tip over and capsize."

WELL CONGRESSMAN JOHNSON, you, Barack Obama and your ilk are the reason for this chapter. For eight years under President Obama, our foreign policy was a disaster. While this is a very complicated matter, in the interest of simplicity we will address it from a macro level. Let's look into some of the biggest foreign policy mistakes America has made and learn how to not make them again, most of which involve some sort of regime change attempt with a half-in efforts. So let's learn from this.

1961, THE BAY OF PIGS

While President Kennedy inherited the plan from his predecessor, he allowed the CIA to carry out this botched attempt at regime change in Cuba anyway. The result was catastrophic, undermining America's resolve in the Cold War. The CIA sent in a small number of troops, less than 1,500 commandos stormed Cuba and were stopped in their tracks. The remainder of air support and Naval resources were called off and most of the commandos were captured and some were killed. This led to the Soviet Union becoming more closely aligned with Cuba and bred the Cuban Missile Crisis. While it has been more than half a century since this event, it still bears a lesson learned. Commit the proper resources, don't do a half-baked effort and once in, stay the course.

1964 – 1975, VIETNAM

We didn't quite learn our lesson in Cuba so four years later we jumped into Vietnam. Let me preface this by saying that great men and women served honorably in this effort. All the credit of honor and bravery is due to those who answered the call, responded to the draft or volunteered in this war. Where the blame lies is on those who developed the strategy or lack thereof. The intent was to halt the spread of communism and reunify the democratic south with the communist north Vietnam.

The result: We lost. Vietnam was in fact reunified under the North's communist rule. Nearly 60,000 American's lost their lives[1] with countless more wounded. America had no further formal diplomatic ties with the country and we divided our own nation at home between the neo-cons and hippies.

But why? Again, despite the massive effort, we underestimated our enemy and did not put forth the necessary resources to obtain victory. Sure, it is easy for us to say that now, but at the time many military leaders said the same thing and President Johnson, seeing the resistance at home to the war effort, compounded by his plunge in approval rating, wavered in his commitment. Through President Nixon and President Ford, we stayed at the table with half-hearted military efforts, but ultimately Congress defunded the effort and the war was ended.

1993, MOGADISHU, SOMALIA

Next is the Black Hawk Down fiasco in Somalia. In the early nineties, George H.W. Bush —and then Bill Clinton—sent resources to Somalia, which was war torn, impoverished and a "shithole" to use a popular buzzword. The effort was well intentioned, but it was clearly not in America's national interest. We tried to help the local populous by providing resources to those in need. The reality, much like the path we saw over the decades in the Middle East, was that we didn't understand the full dynamic of power. President Clinton sought to work with warlords in an attempt to bring relief and peace. In return, local tribes attacked the US forces in Mogadishu, killing or wounding almost one hundred US troops. This was later made into a movie by Ridley Scott.

2003 – PRESENT, IRAQ

Having fought in this war, dropping out of college to join the fight, I believe we began correctly. But again, not learning from history, the US abandoned the fight in favor of nation building, ultimately pulling out all together and resulting in the surge of ISIS.

We supported Saddam Hussain beginning in the early eighties, building an ally in the region to prevent Iranian influence from spreading west. Between then, Desert Storm and 2003, things got really complicated. The debate about weapons of mass destruction is another thing, but going in under that pretense, we started with the right strategy. We walked over the world's fifth largest army in five days, taking key cities like Baghdad, Fallujah and Mosul to remove Saddam Hussein.

Ultimately, Iraq has further deteriorated into a war-torn region. This is a region that has been in almost a perpetual state of conflict since the dawn of mankind; we must have known this going in. Saddam Hussein, a murderous dictator throughout the eighties, kept a balance of power that the region and populous needed. When we marched in and tried to hand them Jeffersonian democracy, they were honestly not intelligent enough nor had the cultural desire to embrace or implement it. We didn't do our homework on the culture; the region is more loyal to religion than government, with perpetual conflicts between Sunni, Shiite and Kurds. And after upending their already fragile economy, smashing national and regional utilities, and bombing some of the most established parts of the country, Iraqi people took sides. Some with the US, some with neither, but many with an anti-coalition insurgency.

While I was in Baghdad in 2007, we were killing bad guys, lots of them. That is what you send soldiers in for. But then things changed; fast forward to Barrack Obama who campaigned on ending the Iraq war. When I returned in 2009 to Fallujah, the effort was starkly different. This echoed of the Vietnam withdrawal and many of us in the military saw it coming. President Bush even said:

> *"I know some in Washington would like us to start leaving Iraq now. To begin withdrawing before our commanders tell us we're ready would be dangerous for Iraq, for the region and for the United States. It would mean surrendering the future of Iraq to al-Qaeda. It would mean that we'd be risking mass killings on a horrific scale. It would mean we'd allow the terrorists to establish a safe haven in Iraq to replace the one they lost in Afghanistan. It would mean we'd be increasing the probability that American troops would have to return at some later date to confront an enemy that is even more dangerous."*

Well, he was right. As the withdrawal efforts began, in the increasing absence of conventional forces, my platoon of Navy SEALs was tasked with nation building and training local Iraqi forces. There were plenty of bad guys, we just were not allowed to go kill them because we didn't want to give the appearance of a continued war. Ultimately President Obama claimed victory as he pulled the last troops out, leaving a power vacuum that would reignite the conflict some years later. This is the problem with liberals because they don't understand that the enemy gets a say in whether or not the war is over, and they were obviously not in agreement.

What was the end result? How did we define victory? I recall a conversation I had at Trump Tower during the transition with Mike Flynn and a number of others poised to be senior members of the cabinet. I said "We need to define victory, all in or all out and that call needs to be made prior to recommitting to the fight. We keep losing wars because we don't take the time to understand the local dynamic and run away when approval ratings drop. Fight to win."

I remember clear as day when one of the members in the meeting looked at me and chuckled, "Ok Carl, what do you recommend?"

Maintaining my bearing, I said "We now have a commander-in-chief who is willing to get shit done and is goal oriented. I don't have all the answers, sir, but you should. You have had fifteen years of war to figure it out. Maybe take a page from Mr. Trump's book. When he builds a building, he defines the end result. He knows how many floors, how many rooms, how long it will take and how much it will cost. You should apply the same steps to your initial planning, that's a start."

We started this war with the right spirit, but we lost our way by becoming more concerned with collateral damage and the Iraqi populous than our own troops' lives and the mission.

In all these conflicts we see similarities:

1. A failure to understand the enemy.
2. A failure to see it through.
3. A failure to commit the necessary resources no matter the perception or immediate backlash.

When you fight a war or conflict, the goal should be to win and to crush your enemy, not to nation build. Once the enemy has been destroyed, then you can worry about the next steps, but time and time again we have installed regimes or leaders that almost always come back to haunt us. If nothing else, learn from what we did in Afghanistan in 1979 when we armed the Mujahedeen who came to later be known as the Taliban. They were a fundamentalist Islamic group that we armed to help push the Russians out of the region.

Needless to say, it backfired and now we are fighting them in the Middle East, most notably in Afghanistan, while they use many of the weapons we gave them.

We often fall into a policy of appeasement or tolerance and lose the will to fight. And then what? We end up right back where we started, facing the same decisions again and, inevitably, more conflict.

Ronald Reagan once said:

> *"Let's set the record straight. There is no argument over the choice between peace and war, but there is only one guaranteed way you can have peace—and you can have it in the next second—surrender.*
>
> *Admittedly there is a risk in any course we follow other than this, but every lesson in history tells us that the greater risk lies in appeasement, and this is the specter our well-meaning liberal friends refuse to face–that their policy of accommodation is appeasement, and it gives no choice between peace and war, only between fight and surrender. If we continue to accommodate, continue to back and retreat, eventually we have to face the final demand–the ultimatum. And what then?"*

So, much like how Reagan was elected, people got fed up and elected a real man to put America first. Americans are tired of our representatives selling us out on the world stage, giving billions away only to have those same countries snub their noses at us. For example, we have given billions to Pakistan, but when we were searching for Osama Bin Laden their government neglected to tell us that he was living just a short distance away from the gates of their equivalent of West Point. I would have cut that aid yesterday. We give billions to other countries, too. Mexico is one of them, yet they gawk at us when the President proposed putting up a wall to keep people from entering here illegally. The UN takes billions from us and then condemns us for our declaration of Jerusalem as Israel's capitol.

This is characteristic of many policies that came out of the liberal tank. President Obama's apology tour netted us the lowest respect on the global stage than ever before. Proof? Look at the way he was received in Saudi Arabia when the highest official sent to meet him at the tarmac was the Riyadh governor with just a small entourage. When President Trump arrived, he was greeted by their leaders and a parade featuring our national anthem and a horseback escort carrying the American flag! Why? Because, despite what the media may lead you to believe, the world, with the exception of a few countries, recognizes that we are better off when America is strong and leads from the front.

THE PARIS AGREEMENT

Never mind the irony that this multinational climate agreement that sought to lecture America and imposed harsh restrictions on us is named after a city with so much pollution that just breathing their air is equivalent to smoking almost 200 cigarettes. In 2015 President Obama and almost 190 other countries entered the Paris Agreement. Now you may have heard that pulling out of this was the worst thing in the history of foreign policy. Let's look at what it actually is.

The goal of this agreement was to prevent global warming by two degrees over the next fifteen years or so... ok, sounds good, but how? The jury is still out on how much mankind actually contributes to climate change considering 100,000 years ago the planet was almost completely covered in ice, but I do concede it must have some effect. We must also consider that we are a ball of rock ninety million miles away from our only heat source, spinning at 1,000 miles per hour orbiting at thirty kilometers per second in a vacuum with almost 500-degree temperature variations between sun and shade, but I'm not a scientist. The brilliance of the authors of the accord sought to note that there is no universal standard for countries, every country had different levels of commitment. The Paris climate accord really hurts America through mandates that include cutting our industrial progression and decreasing our emissions by 28 percent; other places like India and China would have little change. It also required the US and a few other countries to give around $100 billion to countries to help them industrialize in a greener fashion to curb their emissions. This doesn't sound fair to me or to the American economy. After pulling out of the agreement, President Trump said, "I was elected to represent the citizens of Pittsburgh, not Paris."

Damn right. He is doing what is best for our country. The crisis of culture here is that the UN and even many American citizens look out from their ivory towers thinking that America owes everyone everything. The reality is we do not. It is good to support other nations but not those that would not reciprocate when given the opportunity, and especially not those who do not support us on the world stage. Donald Trump was elected because people are tired of horrible foreign policy decisions and mindless conflicts that lead to more conflicts. They want America to come first and not apologize for being better than everyone else.

CHAPTER ELEVEN
ENERGY INDEPENDENCE

"Drill, baby, drill."

SARAH PALIN

IN 2014 AMERICANS consumed almost twenty million barrels of oil per day, according to the US Energy Information Administration. What makes this dangerous to our economic stability is that at the same time we only produced about nine million barrels of oil. Oil prices dictate everything, so in effect everything in the US economy is subject to the Organization of the Petroleum Exporting Countries (OPEC) and other oil-producing nations and their governments, most of whom don't like us.

How did we get here? America has not been self-sufficient in oil production since before 1970 and in an effort to continue to grow economically and industrially, we began importing oil at an alarming rate. Because of this dependency on oil and spineless political leaders and left-wing environmentalists who care more about the mating habits of the blue spotted frog than our economy, our country relies too heavily on other nations for oil. This has become a threat to our national security, much like our debt. Our leaders have let America and its economy become vulnerable to corruption by industry lobbyists and liberals.

No matter who the representatives are, they all have been too scared to drill at adequate tempos to meet our needs. This is because nearly every politician is terrified of losing votes if they sign off on building a supply pipeline or an oil rig five miles off the coast of Florida. So many people complain about the potential environmental hazards these projects present that it scares off political support; however, nobody thinks of the potential hazards if OPEC were to cut us off. Ironically, the hippies who cry about a pipeline potentially endangering animals and the environment are the same people that whine about gas prices being too high, like Al Gore. It is also important to note that these same hippies who protested the Keystone Pipeline over environmental concerns left behind 835 dumpsters worth of trash at the protest site.[1] This begs the question of motivation—do they care about the environment or a political agenda?

It has become more politically correct to appear to look out for the environment than it has to actually look out for our economy, and the general electorate had enough this election cycle.

America also has a tendency to be a pushover when it comes to asking other nations for help or even compensation. America militarily occupied Iraq for a decade, and no one thought to take their oil while we were there? Not only were our representatives spineless, they were morons.

The same politicians who are too scared to take advantage of the resources we have on our soil are also the ones pushing for more time and resources to be spent on green energy. No matter how much money you throw at windmills and solar panels, these sources will never be a viable option for our country's energy needs. This will only result in higher energy prices and a lot of dead birds. Government-funded Solyndra scandals won't work either.

There needs to be free market investments and more support for nuclear power plants, which work great and are relatively easy to fuel over long periods of time. And obviously when your left-wing friends tell you that nuclear power isn't safe, don't believe them. They are the same friends who think Al Gore is the environment's hero as he flies back and forth across the country in his private jet.

How do we solve these things? We are freaking Americans. We put a man on the moon, invented the light bulb, the atomic bomb, the internet and silicone breast implants. The government needs to relax the regulations and leave it to the private sector, or better yet compete with the private sector for it. Not only because the government takes the fun and fluidity out of nearly everything, but because they will let personal political agendas stifle innovation. The only thing the government can do is create incentive. If a president went on TV and said, "The first company and its employees to invent a sustainable, affordable and clean energy source comparable to fossil fuel will pay no corporate, payroll or income taxes of any kind for five years," I would bet the farm that within a year there would be some crazy innovations. It would be more productive than the international space race.

Look, it's time to get real about energy self-reliance. Anything else is irresponsible, stupid and in all seriousness, a risk to national security. The initiative would have to start first and foremost with limitations for the government to live by (much like those laid out in our founding documents). The government has more resources than the private sector after they confiscate our profits. They are also in charge of the big organizations that try to change the availability of necessities for the private sector, like the Environmental Protection Agency (EPA). If they were forced to limit consumption of fossil fuel or live by the rules they place on small business, they would find an alternative fuel solution, and if they didn't, the private sector would beat them to it and charge them for it. Either way, someone would come up with it.

While I am definitely not the next Einstein, I was able to research and build a hydrogen generator in my garage for under $100 in less than a day. It produced enough hydrogen volume to run a portable generator for two hours without using fossil fuels and with using just a gallon of water. If I can do it, it should blow your minds that the government with billions of dollars and thousands of ten-pound heads can't. Now, some scream conspiracy theory about oil companies secretly running the show. Yes, this is partly the case; they do make alleged efforts to squash innovation to maintain profits, but so does the government. They do this because, in 2011, the government got about double the profit of the oil companies for every gallon of fuel you bought[2], so why would they want to kill their cash cow?

I'm not saying buy a hybrid car to do your part, because your emissions are hardly affecting the environment. I care about the environment, but I care about people's quality of life more. If you think that you are doing your part by driving a hybrid car consider this: A 747 jet burns about 3,600 pounds of fuel per hour at cruising altitude, and for mathematical ease let's leave out the additional 8,000 pounds it burns just to take off. With more than 400 of the 747 models in service today worldwide, it is a very conservative personal estimate to assume that one hundred fly every day for an average of five hours. So that comes out to about 1.8 million pounds of fuel burned by these aircraft alone. According to the FAA there are between 50,000 and 70,000 flights a day, so by that math 1.8 million pounds of fuel is burned every day by less than .005 percent of the airline industry daily. How many gallons does your hybrid burn compared to someone else's SUV? Not as significant as you thought, is it? Also consider how bad many of the products that go into producing a hybrid car are for the environment, like the batteries.

Right now we are dependent on fossil fuels, and we need to be realistic about the companies that provide them. The big oil companies get all of these tax breaks that liberals try to take away because, ultimately, we the people end up paying for those tax hikes. In capitalism, a concept void in many liberals' minds, when a company incurs more costs they push it onto customers, cut overhead costs or go out of business. Unless they get a government bailout, in which case they take you and me to the bank and still go out of business anyway the next year like Solyndra. With gas costing around $4 a gallon over the last decade, something has to be done.

First, we need to drill here now, then finish the Keystone pipeline yesterday as President Trump ordered. With the recent trend in the cost of fuel, there is a break-even point that on occasion dips below profitability for oil companies, but rest assured that prices will fluctuate, and we need to be ready. Line parts of the coast with oil rigs far enough away to not be an eyesore and jump start the shale oil industry, too. But most importantly, attack OPEC. I don't mean bomb them; I mean give them the proverbial bitch slap. Create a massive drilling initiative domestically that will keep oil below $60 a barrel indefinitely, broadcast it to OPEC and say, "Hey, America is going to stop buying oil from you tomorrow unless you agree to keep the price below $60 a barrel." Imagine the long-term boost to our economy if we were energy self-sufficient, and not to mention long-term fiscal stability of exporting crude oil. But what if they called our bluff? They can't; the US is such a large portion of the market that they would have no choice but to comply. Sure, it's a strong-arm tactic, but only the strong survive in today's market.

CHAPTER TWELVE
IMMIGRATION

STOP ILLEGAL IMMIGRATION: HOW AND WHY OUR GENERATION MUST INSTALL A COMMON-SENSE SOLUTION

"A nation without borders is not a nation."

RONALD REAGAN

"My dream is a hemispheric common market, with open trade and open borders, some time in the future with energy that is as green and sustainable as we can get it, powering growth and opportunity for every person in the hemisphere."[1]

HILLARY CLINTON

"Well look, I voted numerous times when I was a senator to spend money to build a barrier to try to prevent illegal immigrants from coming in."

HILLARY CLINTON

"The wall is getting built."

DONALD TRUMP

AMERICA IS a land comprised of immigrants, with borders and a national sovereignty to maintain. Complicating this fine balance is the stark reality that our economy is tied to immigration, particularly illegal immigration. So how should we balance our immigration heritage with the need to have clear, controlled borders? How do we reform immigration without destabilizing the economy? I slightly disagree with some public fundamentals but agree on the heart of this issue, which is fair and functional immigration policies. I have gotten in trouble in the past for saying that I want to use lethal force to defend our borders; 2013 I didn't say it as elegantly as I will here, as every anchor on CNN so kindly noted, but I still believe there to be some merit on this. In every other country we operate in, if we want to secure a border, wall or territory, we post armed guards with clear lines of engagement. With the threats we face today, our borders, both north and south, should be protected with similar practices, but not without CLEAR warnings. Make it known with signs in English, Spanish, French or other languages not to cross the borders. Plead with people and give fair warning but defend our borders using appropriate force. Otherwise, people will disregard our laws as they do now, and you can't tell me that when people cross the border they don't know what they are doing because they know exactly what they are doing. Mark my words: the mainstream media will not quote this part when they run their hit pieces on me as a heartless militant, but I want it to be known that it is never my desire to use any level of force against people fleeing to seek a better way of life. However, that does not negate the reality of our borders. We need to decide if they truly exist or not.

There are around twelve million illegal immigrants in America, and about half of them are Mexicans, according to Pew Research Center. The Democrats have made a strong stand to support this group not because they actually give a damn about them or their livelihood, but because they see them as a loyal voting class for future elections. This is evident by the fact that many Democrats have advocated that people here illegally should be allowed to vote. Let's be honest with ourselves: if the Democrats thought for one second that the illegal population would vote Republican, they would build the wall twice as high as President Trump wants to.

It is also estimated that every year about 500,000 people cross the border to the United States without authority (illegally). Although those numbers are recently down, that has been the pattern. As the numbers indicate, immigration is an issue that is complex and pressing. Every year the United States sets a low quota of Mexican immigrants that can enter the country legally, but until Donald Trump a soft stance on enforcing the immigration laws meant that excessive numbers entered illegally. Additionally, there are thousands more across the globe attempting to gain citizenship, many of whom have earned advanced degrees from American colleges and university, sometimes even at in-state tuition rates.

Yet another problem is that many illegal immigrants[2] enjoy many of the same liberties as tax paying citizens. Under President Obama, the federal government spent more time and money scolding and opposing those who enforce immigration laws than actually enforcing those laws. Cities like San Francisco and other safe havens or sanc-tuary cities for illegals are not confronted about refusing to enforce federal law, and worse yet, continue to receive federal funding for various social programs. All American citizens should be outraged by this, and during the 2016 elections Donald Trump made it very clear that this is an issue. He cited time and time again the number of crimes being committed by illegal aliens who had been deported before and came back.

And with the large number of illegal immigrants crossing the border comes a large bill. Social Security and Medicare are just a few of the government benefits that illegal immigrants take advantage of, according to a report by Robert Rector and Jason Richwine published by the Heritage Institute. What most people don't realize is when these people are here illegally they are also taking advantage of bene-fits that Americans have to pay for. This includes welfare, public schools and public services, such as the roads, services of police and firemen, etc.

Aside from the illegal immigrants blatantly disregarding our laws, we can't afford to sustain them. According to the Center for Immigration Studies, "Amnesty for illegal immigrants will cause costs to increase significantly ...This is because an amnesty program would transform an illegal immigrant to an 'unskilled immigrant' with legal status." And due to the low income of this demographic, these unskilled immigrants with legal status would likely make very modest tax payments, thus putting an even greater burden on the middle class. Bluntly stated, our federal and state governments are heavily in debt, granting amnesty to these individuals will only increase our financial woes. Additionally, on a Friday, go to a Western Union. There is a line out the door of many people that do not speak English who are most likely here illegally sending money out of our economy that was earned at the expense of it, usually tax free. This plays a part in hurting our economy.

DACA (DEFFERED ACTION FOR CHILDHOOD ARRIVALS)

DACA, while well intentioned, is a roundabout plan for amnesty. Barrack Obama circumvented our existing immigration laws unilaterally to grant certain illegal immigrants a variation of legal status through work visas if they had entered the country as minors. However, this is not in the authority of the executive branch. So, in September 2017, when President Trump told Congress they had six months to deal with it and that he would do away with President Obama's executive order, he was complying his constitutional mandate to "faithfully execute the laws as passed by Congress", unlike his predecessor. The media will have you think that these are ten-year-old children being ripped out of their parent's arms and it is all President Trump's fault for enforcing the law. The reality is that most of these so-called "Dreamers" are in their twenties and thirties. It is not the president's call, that belongs to Congress and they have had years to deal with this, but they haven't. It is their fault and even when the left has been offered a pathway to citizenship for 1.8 million of the "dreamers" with the contingency that they would build the wall, they denied it. When do they start looking out for Americans? Our economy cannot sustain the amnesty that the left wants, but they know this, too, and seem not to care.

PENALTIES FOR EMPLOYERS

"But my view is that you need a system at the border. You need some fencing but you need technology. You need boots on the ground. And then you need to have interior enforcement of our nation's immigration laws inside the country. And that means dealing with the employers who still consistently hire illegal labor."

JANET NAPOLITANO, FORMER ARIZONA GOVERNOR

If amnesty is not the solution, what is? We need to find illegal immigrants, deport them and don't let them back in.

In order to discourage illegals from coming here in the first place, we have to limit their ability to prosper domestically, after all that is why people come here. Sites like E-Verify.gov, where employers can check the eligibility of their employees, is a good start. Liberals can call it discrimination or whatever they want, but everyone should want programs like that to keep American jobs in the hands of American citizens so that their profits go back into the American economy. The more money that goes into our economy, the more people will compete for transactions...meaning, drumroll... that prices will be lower for the consumer. Some people cry "who will cut my lawn?" Well I owned a tree service that had a landscaping division. Every person in that company was a legal employee. So, stop whining, leftists, Americans *will* cut your lawn.

ANCHOR BABIES AND CHAIN MIGRATION

"All persons born or naturalized in the United States, and subject to the jurisdiction thereof, are citizens of the United States and of the state wherein they reside," according to the Fourteenth Amendment of the United States Constitution.

While I fancy myself a bit of a constitutionalist, I believe that we may need another amendment to prevent illegal immigrants from giving their children US citizenship by jumping the fence and giving birth. This prevents the kind of back-door citizenship that is being granted. The fact is, by current interpretation, if a non-American jumps the fence to our side and pops out a child on US soil, that child is techni-cally an American citizen.

In order to claim citizenship, you should prove that your parents were here legitimately. No more anchor babies. This way, we can send the entire family back without the family claiming citizenship for an anchor baby. No more medical treatment, no more aid and certainly no amnesty. Some may think it's cruel, but far fewer people will jump the fence just to have a child if they know they are going to be shoved right back across the fence with their baby.

Chain migration is not much different. Currently being taken advan-tage of is the ability for people to come into our country and bring family with them that would otherwise not be allowed here legally. This is chain migration.

BORDER SECURITY

Let me preface this by saying that we need to streamline our citizen-ship process; that alone will drastically reduce the number illegal immigrants. But if you are going to come to the United States, it has to be on our terms and benefit us. This could mean quotas, limita-tions and other restrictions, but just because you are having a hard-ship in your country does not entitle you to enter the United States.

Most paramount to our immigration problem is border security. We need to build two fences, the first one six feet high on the border, then one twenty feet high that is 300 yards into the American side. The outer fence would have signs in Spanish and English with our terms and warnings. The sign would read:

This fence marks the border between America and Mexico. If you cross this fence you will be subject to lethal force.

If you crossed, you could be subject to that force by American military and/or militia that would occupy guard stands for the entire length of the border. I hate that I have to suggest this, but we are facing global threats and the security of my country is more important than illegal immigration, so we need real solutions to issues threatening our sovereignty. I hope that we would never have to use force, but it is an unfortunate reality and this is why we have a military in the first place.

Trust me, just the idea of a hardline policy will help those trying to enter our country illegally to understand that the United States is no longer going to accept invasion. Illegal immigrants know that what they are doing is illegal, but they do it anyway because the laws are not consistently enforced. With a policy like this, I can guarantee there will be a drastic decrease in the number of people jumping the border illegally.

For the screaming liberals losing their minds, I would ask that if you have a problem with this proposal then remove your front door and start handing out free food to anyone who comes in. Let them sit on your couch and sleep in your bed and if one of them commits a crime in your home, let them stay. Sound ridiculous? It is, but that is exactly what the left is proposing on a nation level.

REFORM IMMIGRATION POLICY

Finally, our generation must work to make legal immigration easier. As it stands now, legal immigration is extremely difficult and time consuming. Those who wish to immigrate to the United States face mountains of paperwork, years of waitlists and a tedious navigation through bureaucracy and red tape. Our generation should streamline the immigration process.

Of course, the immigrant would need to pass a background check and the standard immigration test, but once completed, let's open the door. Let's get those immigrants here on US soil and let him or her open a business or use his or her skills to contribute to our economy and collect tax dollars from income earned. And let's have foreign students stay in the United States once they have earned an advanced degree from one of our universities. If you get a doctorate, MBA or the like, I want to staple a green card to that diploma because I want to keep you here to innovate in our country.

But with these grants of citizenship, we need to have some conditions such as a five-year probation period. If you commit a crime during that five-year period, then you are deported. If you are affiliated with Islamic extremists, then you should be deported.

By providing immigrants with more realistic and quicker paths to citizenship, our generation could greatly reduce illegal immigration.

Some may think these suggestions are harsh, but it is time to start looking out for America and our future, first. Again, our generation must stop worrying about who is offended and worry about who is affected. By reforming our immigration policy and taking a tougher stance on illegal immigration, our generation can promote legal immigration and greatly reduce illegal immigration.

PART FIVE

THE MANDATE

GENERATION Y'S MISSION TO SAVE
AMERICA: RESTORING THE
CONSTITUTION, THE SOCIAL ISSUES,
WAR, DAYCARE FOR ADULTS, AND THE
LEFT'S USE OF THE INTERNET TO
BRAINWASH US

CHAPTER THIRTEEN
RESTORE THE CONSTITUTION

WHY WE MUST RESTORE THE CONSTITUTION

---

*"*There is nothing stable but Heaven and the Constitution.*"*

PRESIDENT JAMES BUCHANAN

FROM THE DAYS of the *Magna Carta*, the English have waged a battle to limit government power and provide protection for individuals against the tyranny of centralized power. The product of the English struggle was the United States and our Constitution, and in particular, the Bill of Rights. James Madison's mission for "We the people...to form a more perfect union" resulted in the world's most splendid and nearly perfect document.

From America's bedrock document, early Americans were afforded the opportunity to live free of overburdening centralized government control. Through that freedom we built businesses and an industrial and financial empire that leads the world. We research and develop cutting edge technology. We create world-class art and literature. The United States Constitution serves as an example to peoples and nations all over the world who seek to limit the power and possible oppression from government and live in freedom and liberty.

But since the era of the New Deal, those on the left have eroded the Constitution. The president and Congress have passed legislation that far exceeds the powers originally granted to them (as we covered with DACA) and have greatly inflated the size of the government to a ridiculous amount. Supreme court justices have wrongly interpreted the meaning of the Constitution, allowing for health care legislation to be pushed through that opened the door to a single-payer style form of socialized medicine, something the framers never contemplated, among other things. Our nation is in a mess, and largely because the establishment on both sides has perverted the original meaning and intent of the Constitution.

This is all rooted in the fact that most people don't know anything about the Constitution, as CNN so kindly pointed out in an article on the University of Pennsylvania's Annenberg Public Policy Center.[1] More than one in three could not name a single right protected by the First Amendment. Only one in four can name all three branches of the government. A third of the country can't name *any* branch of government. There was a litany of other questions asked but those illustrate that crisis of constitutional culture we are experiencing. How do we bring that back?

We must put an end to the notion that the Constitution can be interpreted in many different ways and changes its meaning with time. The Constitution is very clear in its meaning and is not meant to be interpreted any differently. As President Andrew Johnson said, "Honest conviction is my courage; the Constitution is my guide." How can we have a guide if that guide is constantly changing? There are ways built into the Constitution to change or amend it but when our leaders, especially Barrack Obama disagreed, they change the narrative and boldly lie to the American people and do it anyway. The left has said that we should interpret the Constitution with the framers' intentions in mind. Our framers had their children carry their guns (the same guns carried by the military) to school, should we do that? No? So let's agree to take it at face value.

But my generation faces an uphill battle. The left loves spreading the myth that our Constitution is a "living" document because power-hungry politicians love the idea of bending and molding the Constitution in order to carve out more power. True leftist revolutionaries wish to destroy, or at least minimize, the Constitution in order to push through a radical leftist agenda. After all, who can stop sweeping socialist "reforms" when the Constitution is too weak to stop the trend?

I am not saying that the Constitution is dead, but I am here to say that it is not "living" as the leftists want you to believe. To stop the nonsense, our generation must read the Constitution with an eye toward the framer's original intent. Those in the judiciary who take such a view are called "originalists," or sometimes, "Federalists" as the Federalist Society promotes such a reading. The left tries to paint these groups as extremists in order to discourage people from thinking this way. It is not extreme to read the Constitution as is. The Constitution is not an objective piece of art hanging up in a museum that people can interpret anyway they feel at the time. It is a document that gives us the promise of freedom and a good life, and this can only be done with less government control. My generation is faced with the task of restoring this interpretation, the right interpretation, as written.

We can start by addressing Article I, Section 8. This section lays out the *enumerated* powers of Congress. I stress "enumerate" because the framers felt it necessary to list the specific powers of Congress to limit the power of the federal government. Common sense would dictate that if Congress had unlimited powers to regulate the states and citizens, no list would be necessary.

In Section 8 we find our most abused powers, such as the Commerce Clause, the Tax and Spend Clause and the General Welfare clause. New Deal legislation came about and greatly expanded the role of the federal government. Then the Supreme Court decided to open the floodgates to federal legislation when it ruled that the federal government could legislate what an individual farmer produced on his own land—even if he never sold the produce in interstate commerce. Don't believe me? Read 1942's Supreme Court case *Wickard v. Filburn.*

The federal government recognized a power vacuum via interpretation and began to systematically fill that gap with overreaching legislation—legislation that Alexander Hamilton would have deemed unconstitutional. In fact, Hamilton wrote in "The Federalist No. 33" that any congressional act not specifically within the enumerated powers of the Constitution was an "act of usurpation" which "deserves to be treated as such." Today the federal government consistently abuses their powers with no consequences.

If you still think of yourself as free and feel that the Constitution is safe, think again. The varying interpretations that the Supreme Court and government have convinced you are right have allowed for large violations of the Constitution right under your nose. Again, think about Obamacare and many of President Obama's executive orders on immigration. Our Constitution is being destroyed right before our eyes, and President Obama got away with it because he convinced you that the Constitution is a "living" document.

In Article 1, Section 8 of the Constitution it states, "The Congress shall have power to lay and collect Taxes, Duties, Imposts and Excises, to pay the Debts and provide for the common defense and general Welfare of the United States; but all Duties, Imposts and

Excises shall be uniform throughout the United States." Our founding fathers knew the importance of individual rights and knew that without individual freedoms a society was not free. To protect the "general welfare" of American citizens is to protect their individual freedoms, not to provide them with free stuff.

But unfortunately, the latter definition is basically how it is interpreted by the Supreme Court, which thinks of it as the ability to use federal funds if it supports the best interest of the general public. This is just wrong, and James Madison foresaw this interpretation and said so, "If Congress can employ money indefinitely to the general welfare, and are the sole judges of the general welfare, they may take the care of religion in to their own hands; they may appoint teachers in every State, county, and parish and pay them out of the public treasury; they make take in to their own hands the education of children, establishing in like manner schools throughout the Union; they may assume the provision of the poor... Were the power of Congress to be established in the latitude contended for, it would subvert the very foundations, and transmute the very nature of the limited government established by the people of America."

Madison envisioned a terrifying world where the federal government could take taxpayers money and pay for welfare programs and a Department of Education. That world doesn't seem as terrible to us because that is the world we live in, but to think that where we are now is nowhere near where the founding fathers intended us to be should be a reality check for many.

As Ron Paul has stated, "the language of the Constitution never suggested that 'the general welfare' clause and the 'interstate commerce clause' could even hint at justifying a federal welfare-warfare state. Yet over the years, especially since the Great Depression of the 1930s, a 'modern' interpretation was forced on us by our courts and taught in our schools. This meant that the Constitution could be changed at will by the three branches and without proper amendments...."[2]

The establishment has also vastly expanded executive power, and this should greatly concern my generation considering the founding generation intended the executive to hold the least amount of power and Congress to hold the most. After all, Congress has the power to tax, spend, decide the issue of war, print money and regulate trade. Today, these functions have largely been ceded to the executive branch at least in influence.

Take for example the power to wage war. The War Powers Act of 1972 has afforded the president the ability to engage our troops overseas for ninety days without congressional approval. Absurd! First, a war can be started, fought and won or lost within ninety days, thus totally cutting the power from Congress. Second, and more pragmatically, what congressman would vote to cut funding for the war or withdraw troops once the president has deployed them? Congress is stuck in a lose-lose situation because, in a very real sense, the president has usurped the war-making power from Congress.[3]

The executive power abuse also entails executive orders. This slick maneuver allows the president to issue an order to theoretically apply to the execution of laws by the executive branch. Although the power is rooted in the Constitution's authority for the president to "take Care that the Laws be faithfully executed" (Article II, Section 3, Clause 5), the power constantly receives abuse. Again, see DACA. These are blatant abuses of power, but people have been brainwashed to think that they are just new interpretations of a document that only has one meaning.

When the Constitution was written it included this set of rules to protect against the executive branch abusing its power, but it was made clear that in the end it was really the states that held all of the power, not Congress or the president. When the states retained these powers, they set themselves up to serve a bulwark against a possibly expanding and overwhelming federal government.[4] Sound extreme? It didn't sound that way to our first chief justice, John Marshall, when he said, "No political dreamer was ever wild enough to think of breaking down the lines which separate the States, and of compounding the American people into one common mass."[5]

News flash liberal America: we are called the "United States" for a reason, we are a nation comprised of states. People live in different states for many reasons other than scenery. We are a diverse nation and our states should reflect that quality. In other words, different states should and do have different rules, policies and regulations. Simply stated, we're a federation.

Our founding fathers feared and abhorred centralized power because they fought to get away from a monarchy, so they created a federation to decentralize it. They created a federal government to handle the political needs of a nation such as handling foreign diplomacy, national defense, issuing currency, and so forth. These "enumerated" powers, those specifically given to the federal government, and given to the federal government by the states when they created it, are and were those powers that *needed* to belong to the national government. Those powers not critical to the national government were to remain with the states. It's a very simple and important concept, but the left will tell you otherwise.

Many founders believed this notion was so easy to understand that they did not even believe a Bill of Rights was necessary. Others, ever fearful of a power-hungry government, called for a Bill of Rights and hence, one was drafted. Contained in the Bill of Rights is one of the most important of all our rights, the Tenth Amendment. Never heard of it? This may be so considering the left does not exactly advertise it and it has been largely suppressed in our education system, that is federalized by the way.

Just as we must limit executive power to that power intended by our founding fathers, we must also restore the power and importance of the Tenth Amendment. Under the Tenth Amendment, states have the right to retain all powers not explicitly granted to the federal government.

The Tenth Amendment needs no interpretation because it clearly states, "The powers not delegated to the United States by the Constitution, nor prohibited by it to the States, are reserved to the States respectively, or to the people." We would assume that this amendment would allow the states to make their own decisions on health care, abortion, marriage and a myriad of other issues not expressly covered in the Constitution—in fact, every issue not specifically listed in the Constitution. So why is this line blurred? By this logic, it says states have the right to legalize marijuana, but does not give states the rights to have their own firearm restrictions, that is left to the federal government, but there is no national concealed carry permit.

This has numerous benefits. The framers greatly limited the power of federal government, thus attempting to keep power with the states and local governments. As James Madison wrote in "The Federalist No. 45", "The powers delegated by the proposed Constitution to the Federal government are few and defined. Those which are to remain in the State Governments are numerous and indefinite. The former will be exercised principally on external objects, as war, peace negotiation, and foreign commerce...The powers reserved to the several states will extend to all the objects, which, in the ordinary course of affairs, concern the lives, liberties and properties of the people, and the internal order, improvement, and propriety of the state." Again, it's a pretty clear-cut rule.

As scary as it is to see the abuse of power by the executive branch and the federal government, with clear and public violations of our Constitution, 2015 saw some of the worst attacks on the First and Second Amendment as well. Today universities have areas on campus called "free-speech zones" where students have the chance to say whatever they want. I thought that the entire country was a free-speech zone thanks to the First Amendment, but I guess that is no longer the case. And during the last year of Barack Obama's presidency the war on guns became a disaster. With every shooting in a gun-free zone you can count on the left to call for more gun control, wanting more and more people in this country to be left defenseless. Both of these amendments are vital to our freedom and safety, and as they get pushed around, so do we.

But examine the logic of the argument on banning guns due to a shooting. Do we hold spoons accountable for fat people or cars responsible for drivers killing people? The left screams that you cannot hold a whole religion responsible for a few Islamic extremists, but why can you do it for gun owners? I have no statistics to back this up, but I would be willing to make a healthy wager that as a group on a percentage basis, NRA members are more law abiding than registered Democrats... Prove me wrong.

I have these debates all the time with liberals who ask if I am open to some compromise on assault weapons. No, I'm not! Why? Because I don't have to. And it is not a compromise they want because they want law-abiding gun owners to give up a section of their liberties for nothing in return. That is not a compromise. A compromise would be where both sides give something. Me giving up a significant number of guns in my arsenal for their shortcomings in knowledge does not help solve any shooting problems.

Our government has ripped the Constitution to shreds in the last couple of decades and it is time for us to start patching it up. The problem is that most people just don't understand what it is. We must demand the judiciary adopt an originalist philosophy and, more importantly, insist that educators teach that the Constitution is in fact, "dead." After all, a living Constitution means the death of our freedoms. Further, we must limit government power by insisting that the enumerated powers of Congress be interpreted strictly and demand that the Tenth Amendment be adhered to. The government thinks of the people as such mindless robots that they don't even try to hide their abuse of power anymore because they know they'll get away with it. This should piss you off and convince you to get up and do something about it. It is only through our commitment to the Constitution that we can restore it and in turn, restore America.

CHAPTER FOURTEEN
CALLING A TRUCE IN THE
SOCIAL ISSUES WAR

IN APRIL 2012, former Senator Rick Santorum was surging in the polls and appeared to be closing in on the former Governor Mitt Romney. Then, all of a sudden, Rick Santorum's campaign lost momentum. Prior to his home state of Pennsylvania's primary election, he permanently suspended his campaign. What happed? In a nutshell, Rick Santorum focused too extensively on social issues.

Mr. Santorum's downfall in the primary can be attributed to his devout devotion to conservative social causes, and this is not unique to him. Other Republican candidates have also found themselves unpopular because of this. Too often they make gay marriage, abortion and other social causes the focal point of their campaigns. Yet, hypocritically, the Republicans champion states' rights and limited government. Why then do they constantly bang the drum of social conservatism? This adherence, this love-affair with the Moral Majority has cost us millions of voters and countless of elections.

The left has won this battle; they have made this an emotional issue rather than a logical one. It is easy to control opinion and garner votes based on emotion rather than logic. And we as conservatives fall right into their trap by trying to reason with emotion. Have you ever fought with your wife about her parents? No matter how right you are factually, you are wrong because there is the emotional connection that supersedes the reality most of the time. When you look at it through this prism you can see why conservatives lose. Imagine if for just one election cycle abortion was not championed by the Democrats? I would wager that it would be a 10-point swing in favor of Republicans.

Instead of focusing on social conservative issues, the right would find itself much more popular if they stressed the importance of states' right to decide and left it at that. Society's feelings on social issues comes from the morality of the population, and frankly social issues should be decided locally. It isn't the federal government's place to be discussing these things, and the Republicans are doing themselves and our country an injustice when they continue to pretend like they should have any power over social issues and, really, it's hypocritical to their beliefs. The focus should go back to real issues, such as the economy, foreign policy and immigration. Let the left waste time and resources discussing abortion, gay rights and marijuana.

The first example of how this would work for the right can be found in the ever-popular abortion issue as we discussed in the Battle-grounds section. The issue of abortion drives the religious right more than any other issue, with gay marriage only a distant second. The pro-life camp believes abortion is murder. The pro-choice group believes that a woman has rights over her reproductive system, and somehow if you're not able to abort a fetus that means your rights are taken away. The debate is ongoing, yet with *Roe v. Wade*, the legal resolution will be found only in the US Supreme Court, but the emotional war will always rage on.

Until the Supreme Court receives another case—or more accurately, accepts another case—we are in a virtual stalemate, yet we continually fight this battle over and over again, election season after election season. By doing so, Republicans frighten off some women voters who fear they would be forced into the proverbial back-alley abortion if the Republicans got their way. Worse, we divert attention away from our positions on taxes, forging policy and other pressing issues.

Our generation should remember the wise words of Thomas Jefferson who said, "Government is best which governs least." We must understand that part of living in a limited government nation is that no one person can control the free choice of others. If you believe abortion is morally wrong, as I do, then do not have your unborn child aborted. After all, morality is about doing what one perceives as the right thing; not that thing which the government dictates you do or do not do.

As for gay marriage, for largely the same reasons as the abortion issue, our stance on this subject makes us seem unattractive to the gay community and those who prefer limited government. Case in point: because of how Republicans have historically campaigned, Donald Trump was protested at gay pride events despite the fact that he is pro-gay, in fact much to the dismay of his religious Republican base. Conservatives have already lost the same-sex marriage battle culturally and legally. I have made comments in the past myself regarding gay marriage, I have since evolved. I still don't care for the concept of homosexuality, but I do not seek to limit it. I actually have a few friends who are gay, we don't talk about it and laugh about other stuff over a beer. If conservatives want to win this battle we won't be doing so with the government, but, like everything else that needs to be fixed, without it. Issues like this do not belong in the hands of politicians, and certainly not at a federal level, they belong to society to decide what is right and wrong.

I say that we have lost the culture war on this issue because generally society has accepted gay marriage now that the government has made a decision on the issue, with Kim Davis as the exception. The left has succeeded in indoctrinating our society into thinking that somehow those in government know better what is right and wrong, and whatever they say must be accurate and everyone just needs to fall into line. So the government says same-sex marriage is a right, and that somehow means that as a society we must think so to, but what has been forgotten is that the beliefs of the government and the people do not necessarily need to correlate. Not accepting it does not make you a bigot.

After the 2015 Supreme Court decision on gay marriage people were using the hashtag "love wins." Our culture and government are now so blended together that people have the delusion that this decision meant the government cares about love. To the government, marriage is not about who you love, it's about who you decide to join with to have children. If conservatives want to have a fighting chance in the same-sex marriage argument, the government needs to be removed from the equation so that they can start teaching their children the benefits of only having men and women marry without the government contradicting them. And this should start with Republican candidates who understand this and don't spend much time on the issue.

Finally, the Republicans should and must waive the white flag on the war on weed. This war is a waste of taxpayer dollars and is simply not something that the government actually has a say on; people do it so widely that the law is almost irrelevant. It is federally illegal now and people still do it. I am not saying legalize all drugs, but we must find a compromise here.

All of the social issues championed by the Republicans, whether they be the above we just mentioned or others, detract from the message of limited government and states' rights that is the bedrock of our party. My generation, both Republicans Democrats, demand that we call a truce on these red-herring issues and focus all our political attention to the most pressing of matters—of which there are plenty.

CHAPTER FIFTEEN
UNIVERSITIES AND INDOCTRINATION

THE NEW DAYCARE FOR YOUNG ADULTS, WHERE RACE MATTERS AND WORDS HURT

"If you are not a liberal at 20 you have no heart, if you are not a conservative at 40 you have no brain."

WINSTON CHURCHILL

FOR YEARS the left has controlled college campuses, and now the monsters they created have started to step into the workplace and standardize this behavior. In 2015 universities saw a new low as students claimed injustice on campuses across the country. Walkouts, hunger strikes, protests and a list of demands that included resignations from top administrators were happening at colleges across the country. Instead of students opening up a book and reading about real injustice in history, they were pretending it was happening to them and then pouting about it on social media. When students weren't protesting they were hiding in their safe spaces with their blankies and writing down a list of words that triggered them. But the left asked for this when they decided to indoctrinate the youth of America; now we all have to deal with the consequences.

If you had followed what was going on at Missouri University in the fall of 2015 you know exactly how bad universities have become, if you can even call them that anymore since they are more like daycares for young adults. Black students claimed that racism was alive and well on their campus, and to combat it the black football players refused to play, a student refused to eat, and a swastika was drawn in feces in a dorm bathroom. Students on campus even staged a walk out as a form of protest, with students from places like Ithaca College, Yale University and Amherst College walking out to "stand in solidarity" with black students in Missouri. This ridiculous chain of events resulted in resignations from the president and chancellor of these respected university. Why? To appease these mobs. Literally nothing changed and nothing was solved, but it was a chance for a few people to act out and try to get a figure of authority to step down for doing their job. It was a win for mob-rule.

Adding to the madness, during all of this it suddenly became popular for black students to tweet out their experiences on college campuses. These students claimed things like white students would move seats if a black student sat next to them, white students held their bags tighter to them if a black student walked by, and that black students would be picked last for group projects because white students didn't want to work with them.

If you are like me, it is hard to believe many of these claims. Did these students go up to white students and ask them if they got up because they didn't like black people, or could they simply have just been leaving? Did they actually see these people grip their stuff tighter? And how do they know nobody wanted to work with them because they're black? Could it maybe have been because they wanted to work with a friend or another classmate regardless of skin color?

Liberal students don't ask these questions because it wouldn't fit in with their agenda.

There has been and occasionally still is real racism in America, but no matter how badly liberals want it to be true, there is not widespread racism anymore. And when the leftist students can't find any current racism to fabricate and complain about, they bring up past injustices so that they have something to cry about. The truth is that actual racism isn't something the left cares about, it's about the rage that can be manifested to evoke an emotional response so the story will sound the best when they are preaching their agenda. The issue is that the left has weaponized racism to the extent that actual racism is not being recognized as it should.

When a friend of mine who is now a prominent reporter was a budding student on the University of Minnesota campus, she was given an assignment to cover a protest organized by a group called Whose Diversity? Apparently some black students had stormed the university president's office with a list of demands and they wouldn't leave until he agreed to everything they wanted. The list of demands was quite long and included things like hiring more black professors and having a gender-neutral bathroom in every building on campus. The president spoke with them and said he would listen to everything they had to say, but that these changes would take time and he couldn't promise that every one of their demands would be met. He warned them that if they stayed after the building closed he would have no choice but to have the police arrest them. The president ultimately gave in to them and pleaded with the group to leave, and he even allowed them to stay a couple of hours after the building closed. Eventually, he had to call the police and have them arrested.

Outside of the building other members of the group who decided not to go inside were waiting, cheering on their fellow members and talking to the press. One black woman, who was not in school and did not have a job, said she liked to be involved in protests like this to fight back against racial discrimination on campus. She said she had attended the university before, and that the climate toward black people on campus was very racist and sexist. When asked, "What was a specific time that you saw racism on campus?" No answer. Asked again "Can you tell me a specific event that happened where you felt someone was treating you differently because of the color of your skin?"

These questions seemed to make her very angry. She stated that she didn't need to prove anything, and that a white person could not possibly understand and wouldn't understand because they are white. If she felt so strongly about there being racism on campus, wouldn't there have been at least one time that she can recall where she was discriminated against because she was black?

Well of course she can't, because such an event does not exist. In all of my research, I found no institutional policy that discriminates against black people on any campus. I did, however, find examples of areas where there are no whites allowed, Muslim only areas, and of course the Harvard discrimination suit for bias against Asians, but I digress. Black people are not treated differently than white students on college campuses to any discernable measure. I am sure there are always a few exceptions, but this is about manufactured outrage to elicit an emotional response. Students are being taught by the left that they are victims, and it's easy for them to play the race card.

Now if I was out protesting any legitimate claim for a cause I believed in, I would have a story to tell of how it personally impacted me. You see it is not the black students or the homosexual students that are being treated unfairly on campuses across the country, but students who are brave enough to admit that they think differently than the rest of their peers and professors on campus. The second you admit to a professor, classmate or the administration that you lean conservative, you put a target on your back until the day you graduate.

I had a similar experience when I attended the University of

Connecticut for a semester back in 2015. I took a US history class that blamed slavery on Republicans, never mind that at the time of the Civil War not a single record reflects that a Republican owned a slave, Grant did own slaves but at the time was not a registered Republican. Also, the Republican Party was founded in the 1854 on the basis of abolishing slavery, hence people who changed parties did not have slaves. My teacher praised people like President Johnson, condemned President Reagan and blatantly omitted significant details about the Constitution and the Bill of Rights. I challenged the teacher that what she espoused was blatantly incorrect and slanted history. The best part about it was when she actually challenged me.

Up until this point I had sat quietly in the back of the class, listening to her slanted views and leftist monologues. Finally, in relation to an off-handed comment about our political system regarding super PACs being a tool of the Republican Party, I raised my hand and said:

"That is blatantly not true. First let me remind you we are in a history class, not political science. All major candidates have super PACs including your precious Bernie Sanders."

Not used to being challenged, she snapped and said, "Well class, look what we have here... someone who is back in school trying to get his degree because he wasn't able to get ahead without it, probably worked a blue-collar job and wants to try to make something of his life."

Ok, if you are as irritated as I was then you will understand my response. "Excuse me, ma'am, you know nothing about me so before you make patronizing statements it would be worth your while to educate yourself, not only on the subject of your comments but the topic in which you are engaging me on. I have sat here for months listening to you bashing Republicans, obviously you speak from little actual experience in the private sector or even government judging by your cushy tenure here at a state university..."

You could see her starting to realize that she may have engaged the wrong person. I continued, "Since you know so little about me let me tell you... I was in college full time, then we went to war because of 9/11. I dropped out, joined the military, became a Navy SEAL and did almost nine years of service, including two tours in Iraq. Then I came home, started two businesses, wrote two books on the topics that you apparently know nothing about, spent the last five years on national television talking about this very topic and now run a super PAC to support the very type of candidate that you are shitting on, so unless you have some actual facts to back up you liberal bullshit then shut up and teach history because that is what my GI-Bill is paying for."

Needless to say, I almost failed that class. This might explain why college students think the way they do. Even President Obama spoke out against the coddling of college students in a September 2015 town hall, and he is one of the biggest violators of our basic rights. But then this question comes up: are we in the middle of another shift of the political left, a much scarier one where all that matters is whether one feels safe or not, and all of our previous societal morals are thrown out the windows?

Right now, the left might outnumber the right at universities, but it doesn't mean we should allow them to win, nor can our country afford the loss. The right can be just as loud if not louder, but our generation needs to stop letting the left intimidate us and to stand up for what's right. If I would have allowed my university to espouse its view and not the facts just to protect the feelings of other students, I would have been doing my country an injustice. When a professor stands up and outright lies to her students in order to push her own agenda and you don't stand up and correct her, you are no longer part of the solution but part of the problem.

The American people are strong individuals who can take a traumatic situation and grow from it. The left wants college students to think that when they are confronted with controversy or offensive language that they should run to their safe space and hide or even apologize. This mentally weakens our society and makes it easier for politicians to control us. Instead, I want every American to feel empowered despite whatever hard situation is thrown their way, because the American people are extraordinary and are not given nearly enough credit for how smart and mentally strong they really are.

It's time for our generation to remind college students just how capable they are, and it is time for conservative students to start standing up for what is right. Right now the left is winning the war on campus, and if the University of Missouri shows us anything of how college campuses will be in the future if this continues, it doesn't look very good. When you have UC Berkley students rioting because a conservative is coming to speak, it is an injustice. Instead of stifling language that liberals deem offensive, no matter how true, we need to embrace it, because that is the only way that we will be able to mold current students into the productive adults we need to secure our rights against the power of the government. It's important to remember that the government doesn't want people to be strong and courageous, they want them to be weak, because it is much easier to take over a group of people who are scared of everything than it is to take over a group of people who are scared of nothing.

CHAPTER SIXTEEN
INFORMATION
DISTRIBUTION

THE LEFT'S TAKEOVER OF SOCIAL
MEDIA AND POP CULTURE TO
BRAINWASH OUR SOCIETY

"Facebook is not your friend. It is a surveillance engine."

RICHARD STALLMAN, PROGRAMMER,
ACTIVIST, FOUNDER, GNU PROJECT AND
THE FREE SOFTWARE FOUNDATION

IN THE AGE OF TWITTER, Facebook, Instagram and Snapchat, our generation is very blessed. In a matter of seconds anyone with a phone or computer is able to find the latest news from the safety of their homes. Frankly, it is amazing that someone is able to sit in their home in America, even most of those in poverty, and with little effort discover the latest that is going on in the Middle East without having to be there. This is just the newest technology that has been brought to you by capitalism that makes our lives easier and more enjoyable every day.

But, this privilege is taken advantage of. There is no excuse any longer for Americans to not be informed of what is going on in the country and the world. Almost everything anyone could ever need or want to know is easily available. Though I cannot say that everyone needs to know as much as is on the internet just because it is easily accessible, it does mean that there is no excuse for voters to be ignorant when they get to the polls.

As Edmund Burke, an Irish statesman and member of the Whig party, said, "Those who do not know history are doomed to repeat it." The perils of socialism and communism are well documented on the internet, yet we still have people who are willing to give it another try in America. Jim Carey, who is worth $150 million, said we need to embrace socialism... Aside from him just being a moron, there is just simply no excuse for this. Socialism has literally NEVER worked.

Even if people choose not to spend their time researching the history of the Soviet Union, all it takes is opening up a news app to see examples of other countries making mistakes in the past. There is no reason for American citizens to not be informed about the Christians murdered in Iraq or the women stoned to death by Muslims in the Middle East. Though it is wise to look to the past, it only takes one look at a couple of current headlines online to know what policies or ideas should not be repeated in our country.

We need to start taking advantage of all the information we have available and to understand the dangers that come along with it. I am not talking about the dangers of online dating or the Craigslist Killer, but the ability to spread misinformation so easily. It makes me sick when I look through my Twitter feed and see my friends sharing articles and information that is simply not true, but that many people will look at and believe with no questions asked.

When the 2015 Planned Parenthood videos were released by the Center for Medical Progress, my leftist friends were upset and hoped to counter these videos by posting lies on their Facebook pages. I scrolled through my feed to see a picture posted by one of my friends with a list of facts about the services Planned Parenthood offers. I read, "3%- Abortion (which receives ZERO government funding)," which was written in bold to standout.

I could not believe this. This was complete propaganda, and there was no source listed to back up this claim. The truth is more than 300,000 abortions are performed each year by Planned Parenthood, which is about 1/3 of all abortions in the country, according to Jamie Bryan Hall and Roger Severino at the Heritage Institute. Also, each woman who comes in to a Planned Parenthood clinic to receive an abortion will most likely receive a pregnancy test, condoms, birth control pills and a STD test, which Planned Parenthood counts as all separate services when they tally it up, even though it was only given to one person. They do this to make it seem like less people are getting abortions but, in reality, a large percentage of their patients are getting abortions, as well as many other services. Planned Parenthood also has received more than 40 percent ($530 million)[1] of their funding from the government in the past, so do not tell me that government funding does not support abortions because if it wasn't for that money Planned Parenthood would barely be able to operate and there would be far less clinics.

After I saw this post I couldn't stop myself from commenting to set the record straight. Shortly after, I was attacked by multiple people for doing so. Apparently, it does not matter if these facts were not completely accurate and they didn't have a source to back them up. All that mattered was the point that was being made, which was women would be dying in the streets because of cancer and black-market abortions if it wasn't for Planned Parenthood.

But the facts do matter, because if the facts are wrong it leads people to believe a lie. I have this argument all the time with people who want to fall back on their opinions; I ask what they are basing that opinion on and they say it doesn't matter because it's their opinion.

Specifically regarding Donald Trump during the election, I would hear; "Well Trump hates black people and immigrants." When I would ask them what they were basing that on they, of course, resorted to the talking points of CNN. When asked if they knew that Donald Trump had actually received the Ellis Island Award[2] or that two of the three women he married are immigrants—of course they did not. Or that he has provided more opportunity in his industry for black people with in his company than most of society does. He was never called a racist until he ran for president, but that is not what the Twittersphere would have you believe.

This is a perfect example of how social media has trained our generation to think or not think via headlines, regardless of the validity— that it is okay to share false information because facts don't matter, what matters is the point one is trying to make. No one questions this, which is sad because there really isn't a point if there is not any factual information to support it. Like Aldous Huxley said, "Facts do not cease to exist because they are ignored." The left has found a way to convince our society to ignore facts, and they use the internet to support their efforts.

Not only is the spread of misinformation and the failure of most to fact check the information they find on the internet helping the political left gain followers, pop culture is indoctrinating our generation and the generations following. Have you ever watched a new television show and noticed how they try to normalize homosexuality, transgenderism, rap culture, etc.? Most will watch this and just assume that there is a large percentage of people in this country who are parts of these groups. According to a Gallup Poll, in 2012 less than 4 percent of people identified as lesbian, gay, bisexual or transgender in America. So why the push to normalize it?

Why in an episode of *Glee* are so many characters members of the LGBT group when so few of Americans identify as such? Because the left is using pop culture to try to indoctrinate our society into thinking that being gay or transgender is normal. But they do so in such a subtle way that most people don't know that they are being manipulated every time they turn on their televisions.

This tactic is seen in many popular television shows. In *Greys Anatomy*, a show that has been running for more than ten years, multiple scenes tout the liberal agenda and it's painful to watch. In one scene a character was shouting the benefits of Obamacare, and in another a black woman was telling a white woman about the struggles of being black and how white people should "check their privilege." In the show *Scandal* the main character had an abortion to the song "Silent Night." To someone who can recognize this propaganda, there is little impact, but to the millions of people who don't, this can have a disastrous effect.

If this doesn't worry you, it should. I am not trying to make Americans, and specifically my generation, sound dumb for being so easily brainwashed because I do not think they are, but the liberal machine does. Instead of being offended by what you are being called, how about calling out the left that thinks that the majority of the population is so mindless that all they have to do is insert their views into popular television shows and people will believe it. That is propaganda. What comes to mind is a book like *The Poisonous Mushroom* that was given to kids by the Nazi's to subtly encourage the hatred of Jews. If this sounds like an extreme comparison, you do not understand how the dire the situation is.

Sadly, this doesn't end in Hollywood. The mainstream news sources also have a hand in molding the political views of the public. Isn't it strange that CNN or MSNBC weren't critical of the Obama administration's shortfalls? Or that huge stories like the Fast and Furious scandal and the Lois Lerner and IRS scandal were not largely investigated? Could you imagine if Donald Trump were to be involved in something like that? Look at the media coverage when he gets two scoops of ice cream! You would think he nuked a school. Look at the whole Russian collusion story despite ZERO evidence to support it. This was fabricated by the Clinton campaign and sold to a FISA court based on a dossier by a foreign agent paid for by the Trump campaign that colluded with high-level officials in an attempt to destroy President Trump. Then the mainstream media all but convicted the Trump administration despite all of the evidence to the contrary. That is because the left and their celebrity and media cohorts have their own agenda. Most journalists might as well consider themselves part of the fourth branch of government at this point because when they misreport facts or leave out information about the government they are basically working for them.

Since the media refuses to cover it, let me lay out the other side that they didn't cover in this recent line of collusion and government corruption. Now stay with me because it involves all of the players I mentioned above. My inspiration to collect the information below was based on an anonymous reddit article that I independently verified through exhaustive research:

From 2001 to 2005 there was an ongoing investigation into the Clinton Foundation due to the overwhelming money that was brought in from governments from around the world that had donated to the "charity." The investigation found that from 2001 to 2003 none of those "donations" to the Clinton Foundation were declared. This leads any normal person to believe that there was a reason for hiding such information because that does come at a risk, well for anyone but a Clinton. In 2005 who swooped in to shut 'er down? James Comey at the US Department of Justice. Coincidence? Guess who simultaneously was transferred into the Internal Revenue Service to run the Tax Exemption Branch of the IRS? Yup, Lois Lerner. Remember her, the woman who oversaw the targeting of Tea Party groups and the discrimination against their 501c3 statuses? This all looks overwhelmingly biased and corrupt, but guess who ran the Tax Division inside the Department of justice from 2001 to 2005? Drumroll... Assistant Attorney General of the United States

Rod Rosenstein. Oh, but it gets even better, guess who was the Director of the Federal Bureau of Investigation during this time frame? Yup, Robert Mueller. Ok, so now all the folks leading the charge into investigating Donald Trump were all were a part of the investigation into Clinton Foundation that yielded no charges despite all the evidence of pay for play and questionable donations. That might be water under the bridge but go to 2009 under Barrack Obama—James Comey left the Justice Department and got a job way outside his scope of qualifications at Lockheed Martin (a big government contractor).

Hillary Clinton was running the State Department (on a server in her bathroom), and the Uranium One "issue" came to the attention of what appeared to be only Fox News. Hillary Clinton decided to approve the sale of 20 percent of US uranium to the Russians for what appeared to be nothing in return, at least nothing for the American people. So immediately before the sale is approved, Bill Clinton went to Moscow and was paid half a million dollars for a one-hour speech; he then met with Vladimir Putin at his home for a few hours (but Donald Trump is the bad guy for talking to Putin at a public summit). At the same time, the FBI had a mole inside the Clinton scheme. Robert Mueller was still the FBI Director during this time frame and even delivered a uranium sample to Moscow in 2009 personally. Was this a conflict of interest?

So, the Department of Justice takes on the investigation, but who was handling the case from the US Attorney's Office in Maryland? Rod Rosenstein. The Department of Justice placed a gag order on him and threatened to lock him up if he spoke out about it. Recap: 20 percent of the most strategic assets of the United States of America ended up in Russian hands, the FBI had an informant providing inside information, then deferred to the Department of Justice, the informant was gagged by a court order and the sale was approved!

Shortly after, $145 million in "donations" were made to the Clinton

Foundation from entities directly connected to the Uranium One deal. They didn't even try to hide it! That's how blatantly sure the Clintons were that they would not be prosecuted. Let me remind you that Lois Lerner was still at the Internal Revenue Service working the Charitable Division. Pissed off yet?

Remember Benghazi in 2012? In 2015 Trey Gowdy was running the tenth investigation as Chairman of the Select Committee on Benghazi and, for the first time, discovered Hillary Clinton's unclassified, unauthorized personal email server. He also discovered that none of those emails had been turned over when she departed her public service as Secretary of State, which was required by law. He also found (from the emails that were produced and not bleach bitted or smashed with a hammer) that there was top secret information there. Why was Ms. Clinton not worried? Well who had become FBI Director in 2013? It was James Comey, who, by the way, secured seventeen no bid contracts for Lockheed Martin with the State Department and was rewarded with a $6 million bonus when he departed the company. But Donald Trump pays a stripper $130,000 and the sky is falling.

So, Mr. Comey was the FBI Director in charge of the "Clinton Email Investigation" after they investigated the Lois Lerner matter at the Internal Revenue Service. He exonerated her, so she was not about to roll on him. In April 2016, Comey drafted an exoneration letter of Hillary Clinton before the conclusion of the investigation, while the DOJ handed out immunity deals with no exchange of information.

On July the 8th of 2016, Mr. Comey exonerated Hillary Clinton in the email matter (as then-Attorney General Lorretta Lynch requested it be referred to it as). Shocking! Mr. Rosenstein became Assistant Attorney General, Mr. Comey was fired based on a letter by Mr. Rosenstein, Mr. Comey leaked government information to the press, Robert Mueller was assigned to the Russian Investigation by Mr. Rosenstein to provide cover for decades of corruption within the

FBI and DOJ... FISA abuse, political espionage....this is the swamp that President Trump was elected to drain. It's the same names being recycled through different departments and levels of government, all conflicted, all held dirt on each another, but all were getting rich and powerful together. What is the common denominator? Over the last two decades they have all been connected to the Clintons, who oversee the largest international charity in the history of mankind that has never been audited by the IRS.

But look who is on the peripheries. Guess where James Comey's brother works? DLA Piper, the law firm that does the Clinton Foundation's taxes. But more importantly, have you ever heard of Lisa Barsoomian? She is an attorney that graduated from Georgetown Law, a protégé of James Comey and Robert Mueller and long-time insider not far removed from the Clintons. Ms. Barsoomian worked for a man named R. Craig Lawrence, a long-time defender of shady Democrats. While she worked for him she was involved in representing Bill Clinton as president, Robert Mueller three times, James Comey five times, Barack Obama forty-five times, Kathleen Sebelius fifty-six times and Hillary Clinton seventeen times. Now why all of these Democrats constantly need so much representation should beg its own questions, but I digress.

Why is this woman important? Lisa Barsoomian has specialized in opposing Freedom of Information Act requests on behalf of the intelligence community. If you wanted to cover something up, what would you do? Hire the best damn attorney to make sure no one was able to get records of any fraudulent activity officials may have committed. And if you don't think this woman has skin in the game, consider this: she is Assistant Attorney General Rod Rosenstein's WIFE!

The circle of bad actors is so prevalent that in any other world there would be a domino effect, except the corrupt ones have so much power and are now attacking the very people trying to get justice.

Americans can easily fight back against this, and all they have to do is be more aware of what they are listening to, watching and reading. Become knowledgeable so you know what to look for. Instead of taking in everything you see on the internet as fact and everything you watch on television as reality, think about it. Americans are not dumb and need to show the left that they cannot be easily brainwashed. If we are going to solve this Crisis of Culture, people will have to wise up and make decisions on fact, not on emotion. America, it is up to you to not be played by propaganda.

CONCLUSION

"Freedom is never more than one generation away from extinction. We didn't pass it to our children in the bloodstream. It must be fought for, protected, and handed on for them to do the same, or one day we will spend our sunset years telling our children and our children's children what it was once like in the United States where men were free."

PRESIDENT RONALD REAGAN

WE ARE THE FREEST, most prosperous nation on earth. But if we don't wake up soon, the next generation might not have a chance to. Our freedoms and liberties are being taken for granted by people who have never lived without them. My generation has latched onto the progressive left's hatred for America. We are very vocal about all the things we hate, and we don't stop to think how good we have it. We seem to forget the fact that it is *because* our country does not have socialist policies that Americans are free to publicly voice those views without fear of prosecution. America is better than everyone else, maybe not all in measurable statistics, but we are in a uniquely American manner of spirit. The social war we are waging against ourselves is between those who are being told to hate and those that are being told that they are hateful, when frankly the roles could not be more opposite. A large portion of this country is fed up with the divisions and we are dangerously close to an irreparable divide.

There are two sides to choose from in America, right or left, but the mentality that the left is against the right needs to stop. It should not be the people against the government either, because the government works for us, we the people, and it needs to be held accountable. The right is already pitted against the government because we believe in the greatness of the American people. We hear about the "deep state" and it is brushed off as conspiracy. But it is there. A contingent of bureaucrats that will stop at nothing to maintain the status quo, anyone who challenges it will be shot at from every direction, their characters tarnished with real or fake allegations. Much of the media is complicit; the DC beltway voted almost 91 percent for Bill Clinton compared to Donald Trump's 4 percent because they were voting for their own interests and we funded leftist groups that are perpetuating a cycle irresponsibility. President Trump won on "draining the swamp" because we are sick of it and we need to continue the effort.

The two parties have never seen the role of government more differently. To quote *Braveheart*, "You think the people of this country exist to provide you with position. I think your position exists to provide those people with freedom."

And as someone who put my life on the line for this country, I agree with the last line, "And I go to make sure they have it."

The government needs the people, not the other way around, and every single war in the history of mankind has evolved when someone is unjustly oppressed. As I said earlier, our revolutionary war was started over a 2 percent tax hike in tea, what is the next breaking point? Americans are extraordinary individuals, and we need to stop acting like we are incapable of doing anything without the help of the government. Regardless of race or gender, people are capable of thriving on their own, and to suggest that this is only true with the help of the government is insulting.

It is time for our parties to come together and stand up for our rights. We really don't have time to waste because our freedoms are being attacked like never before. With socialized health care, forced amnesty, a large percentage of Americans on welfare, universities violating students' First Amendment rights, and our right to bear arms in jeopardy, among other things, we are seeing the effects of socialism on our shores. This is not the America that our parents grew up in, but this is the only America that our generation knows.

I had a friend who once told me that she doesn't care what laws are enacted, as long as she is told what they are she will follow them.

"If the freedom of speech is taken away then dumb and silent we may be led, like sheep to the slaughter."

GEORGE WASHINGTON

If this complacent attitude continues, we will see our rights taken away one by one, but if we wake up and take action now, before it's too late, we still might have a chance to restore the American way of life.

If we don't act now our future looks dismal, and I am not being dramatic. Look at how people are living in Spain, Italy or Greece. People romanticize Europeans' quality of life, but there is nothing romantic about it. If we continue on this path we can expect a lower quality of life.

"For we must consider that we shall be as a city upon a hill, the eyes of all people are upon us," John Winthrop said in 1630 of the Massachusetts Bay Colony, a destination for those who sought to escape religious persecution in England. The intent of its founders was not to build a nation that would one day rule the world, but rather to build a "shinning city," an example to all of mankind of what the government should and ought to be. In this spirit, William Penn founded Pennsylvania and Roger Williams founded Rhode Island. And not long after, independent experiments in government and freedom sprang up on our eastern seaboard. From Massachusetts to Georgia, shinning little cities that eventually evolved into the **United** States of America.

At her core, the United States has been the most successful experiment of mankind and the goal was to create a nation like no other on earth. A nation of rights and liberties, of justice and rule of law... and we did.

At no point did our founding fathers desire to create an empire nor did they intend for their little experiment, their American republic, to attempt world hegemony.

America is not just a place, it's an idea that individuals can live their lives with freedom and liberty. This idea is under attack and we are the only ones who can stop it. It is time to wake up and start fighting for the America that made us great.

ENDNOTES

WHERE DO YOU STAND ON IDEOLOGICAL FRONTS?

1. https://www.supremecourt.gov/opinions/boundvolumes/528bv.pdf
2. As Joe Biden shamefully said to a predominantly black audience during the 2012 presidential campaign, "They [the Republicans] want to put ya'll back in chains." The Thirteenth Amendment to free the slaves was passed with 100% Republican support with only Democrats opposition.
3. This quote appears on page 155 of Goodwin's *LBJ biography*. The utterance was made to Richard Russell, a fellow Democratic Senator from Georgia.
4. This quote, along with others that show Johnson's true intentions, can be found in Ronald Kessler's book *Inside the White House*.
5. Death Penalty Information Center "Facts about the Death Penalty" 19 July 2012.
6. Death Penalty Information Center "Facts about the Death Penalty" 19 July 2012, citing a Dallas Morning News figure from 1992.
7. US Energy Information Administration, http://www.eia.gov/tools/faq.cfm?id=268&t=6
8. http://www.politifact.com/virginia/statements/2016/apr/04/don-beyer/don-beyer-says-97-percent-scientists-believe-human/
9. A way for the government to turn short-term and/or contrived crises and turn them into permanent government expansion.
10. http://www.skepticalscience.com/volcanoes-and-global-warming-intermediate.htm.
11. Sheople" is a term overheard by a larger-than-life, extremely patriotic, JAG officer from the great state of Texas. He constantly referred to the American population as the "sheople" because they blindly followed the media. The term was quickly coined to describe officers who blindly followed authority. We have started to use "sheople" to describe some in the American public who blindly follow the establishment on either side.
12. https://www.law.cornell.edu/supct/html/07-290.ZS.html
13. For more information see my first book, *Battle on the Home Front: A Navy SEAL's Mission to Save the American Dream* where I quoted extensively from an article written by Kitty Witherman who had firsthand experience with Hitler's gun policy.
14. It is ironic how the left is adamant that health care is a right unsupported by our founding documents, yet so opposed to the right to keep and bear arms when that right is explicitly provided by the Constitution.
15. See Heritage Foundation's Federal Budget in Pictures at http://www.heritage.org/federalbudget/budget-entitlement-programs

16. https://web.stanford.edu/class/e297c/poverty_prejudice/soc_sec/hsocialsec.htm

1. ACCOUNTABILITY AND FAKE NEWS

1. Huntington, Samuel, *The Clash of Civilizations*, Simon & Schuster, New York, NY, 1996, page 304.
2. Thank God the bureaucrats are keeping us safe, right?
3. Why you have to do all this to exercise a constitutionally protected, God given right like carrying a gun, but don't even have to show an ID to vote in most states is beyond me.
4. Another aspect to this case is that of media bias. Besides editing the audio tapes to paint the Hispanic Zimmerman as a racist, the media used photos of Martin from when he was several years younger and smaller.
5. I am not saying to pry into other's personal lives in some kind of puritanical inquisition. What I am saying is that it is time to expect more from each other. It's time to stop making excuses for others and demand accountability.
6. National deficit average has exceeded $1 trillion throughout President Obama's first term, where it tripled during his first year in office.
7. Yes, unbelievably she wasn't immediately fired.

2. PATRIOTISM, SACRIFICE AND SERVICE?

1. http://www.policemag.com/channel/patrol/articles/2016/09/the-2016-police-presidential-poll.aspx
2. http://www.washingtonexaminer.com/harvard-millennials-now-biggest-voting-group-in-us-2-1-democratic/article/2642567
3. Huntingdon, *Clash of Civilizations*, 304.
4. Ok, maybe the Arab Spring started on Facebook, but the young Arabs actually did something to ferment revolution. They protested in the streets and refused to leave public areas until change actually occurred. They didn't post inspirational messages on Facebook and then go to Whole Foods. They acted.

3. MULTICULTURALISM

1. Huntingdon, *Clash of Civilization*, 305.
2. An example of this was in 2009 in New Haven, Connecticut. Twenty white fire fighters sued the state for not being promoted after obtaining scores that made them eligible. The test results were thrown out because no black firefighters had scored high enough to warrant promotion. The city argued, going ahead with the promotions based on the test results would have risked a lawsuit claiming the exams had a "disparate impact" on minorities.
3. I cannot believe I am actually writing this into this book. Fair treatment for all and a merit-based society is the bedrock of the United States.

4. MILLENNIALS...WHAT HAPPENED TO US

1. I understand that I am partially blaming the Baby Boomers for raising what I call "an almost ruined generation." While I believe that Generation Y is ultimately responsible for our own destiny and that the Baby Boomers acted out of love, I believe it necessary to explain how we became the generation we are and what we must do to improve ourselves.

5. FEDERAL WELFARE

1. http://www.heritage.org/federalbudget/budget-entitlement-programs
2. http://www.heritage.org/research/reports/2015/09/poverty-and-the-social-welfare-state-in-the-united-states-and-other-nations
3. http://www.prb.org/Publications/Articles/2012/us-homeless-veterans.aspx
4. http://www.forbes.com/sites/mikepatton/2015/08/31/welfare-spending-by-president-and-congress-from-1959-to-2014/#711f662a3e12

6. OBAMA'S HEALTH CARE DISASTER

1. http://www.foxbusiness.com/features/2013/06/27/outrageous-er-hospital-charges-what-to-do.html
2. http://www.gallup.com/poll/123149/cost-is-foremost-health care-issue-for-americans.aspx
3. http://www.gallup.com/poll/186527/americans-government-health-plans-satisfied.aspx
4. http://kff.org/report-section/ehbs-2015-summary-of-findings/
5. http://www.nationalreview.com/campaign-spot/231091/remember-pelosi-and-bidens-promises-job-creation-jim-geraghty
6. http://www.ncpa.org/pub/ba649

7. REFORM THE AMERICAN TAX SYSTEM

1. http://www.ontheissues.org/Celeb/Ronald_Reagan_Budget_+_Economy.htm
2. http://www.wsj.com/articles/top-20-of-earners-pay-84-of-income-tax-1428674384
3. http://www.washingtonexaminer.com/virginias-tax-me-more-fund-is-a-big-flop/article/5323/section/baltimore
4. http://www.huffingtonpost.com/michael-moore/america-is-not-broke_b_832006.html
5. http://townhall.com/columnists/walterewilliams/2011/04/13/eat_the_rich/page/full
6. http://www.businessinsider.com/income-tax-history-2015-3
7. https://www.sba.gov/.../FAQ_Sept_2012.pdf

8. REDUCE THE FEDERAL GOVERNMENT

1. http://www2.ed.gov/about/landing.jhtml
2. http://energy.gov/mission
3. http://www.washingtontimes.com/news/2015/oct/28/pumpkins-cause-climate-change-energy-department/
4. http://www.dol.gov/general/aboutdol
5. https://www.commerce.gov/page/about-commerce
6. http://portal.hud.gov/hudportal/HUD?src=/about/mission
7. https://www.epa.gov/aboutepa
8. http://reason.com/blog/2015/08/07/environmental-protection-agency-dumps-a
9. http://www.startribune.com/polymet-copper-mine-in-northeastern-minn-gets-cautious-epa-approval/250138951/
10. http://rare.us/story/epa-wastes-taxpayer-money-by-storing-tons-of-old-printed-reports/#sthash.g9wplyWM.dpuf
11. http://www.nytimes.com/2011/08/18/us/politics/18epa.html?_r=0
12. http://www.theguardian.com/environment/2016/feb/26/republican-candidates-donald-trump-eliminate-epa-law-experts
13. https://www.nationalservice.gov/about

9. MILITARY

1. I understand that attention must be paid to officer and enlisted status as well as requisite schooling and certifications to hold various positions. I do firmly believe that free market principal-based hiring would greatly strengthen the quality of our military's leadership and provide incentives for high achieving officers and enlisted personnel to remain in the service.
2. Despite poor performance, many military members never actually receive bad evaluations, even if they are fired from a job. On paper it is looked as though they were simply reassigned. To have a bad evaluation is the kiss of death for any officer, especially one pertaining to failures of leadership.

10. FOREIGN POLICY

1. https://www.archives.gov/research/military/vietnam-war/casualty-statistics

11. ENERGY INDEPENDENCE

1. https://www.washingtontimes.com/news/2017/mar/13/dakota-access-case-army-finishes-11-million-cleanu/
2. http://www.factcheck.org/2011/05/playing-politics-with-gasoline-prices/